YEOMEN
OF THE
COTSWOLDS

A journey of discovery which traces
the history of a Cotswold farming
family back to the 14th century

YEOMEN
OF THE
COTSWOLDS

A journey of discovery which traces
the history of a Cotswold farming
family back to the 14th century

Eleanor Porter & Mary Abbott

IMAGES
PUBLISHING

Best wishes

Eleanor Porter

Published in Great Britain 1995 by
Images Publishing (Malvern) Ltd.,
Upton-Upon-Severn,
Worcestershire.

British Library Cataloguing in Publication Data

A catalogue record for this book is available
from the British Library

ISBN 1 897817 48 7

Set in Gatineau 10pt

Designed and Produced by Images Publishing (Malvern) Ltd.
Printed and Bound in Great Britain by Bookcraft, Bath, Avon.

Contents

A NOTE ON PRICES

Like us, our yeomen of the Cotswolds lived in a money economy. However, while money has been a fact of daily life in England for at least the past four or five hundred years, changes in patterns of consumption, progressive inflation and, for the younger generation of readers at least, decimalisation of the currency, complicate the business of comparing present day prices and values with those of the past. It may be helpful to remind readers that the pre-decimal pound could be broken down into:

* 20 shillings
* 240 pennies
* 480 halfpennies
* 960 farthings

The pound could also be transformed, by the addition of a shilling, into the more stylish guinea.

At the same time, all through the period under consideration, money circulated alongside other forms of currency. Young people living under their masters' roofs received the greater part of their earnings in kind – bed and board and, sometimes, items of clothing; to a lesser extent married men were also paid in kind – when they were fed during the working day, given 'free' milk, a sack of potatoes or a pig to fatten. Trading in kind was common too. Barter did not necessarily occur as a simultaneous exchange of goods or services; perhaps more frequently it took the form of a long and quite complex series of investments and dividends. An individual's credit-rating in the community of farmers and farm workers was determined by reference both to his wealth in monetary terms and to the ease with which he could negotiate favours.

Preface and Acknowledgements

hen I met David Porter's family I realised it was rather different from mine. He was the youngest of nine children, born between 1911 and 1934; his parents Graham and Edith (but never known to us as that of course – always Father and Mother), were the same age as my grandparents and his elder brothers and sisters were a similar age to my parents; but they all welcomed me into the family circle.

Over the years I heard many little anecdotes connected with the family and was always curious to know more. Both Graham and Edith came from farming families, he was one of seven children and she was one of ten, so there were many tales to tell. During the 1970s we had family parties to celebrate Graham and Edith's 60th and 65th wedding anniversaries as well as Edith's 90th birthday. In the summer of 1980, we all gathered to congratulate them on 70 years of marriage, but our next family gathering was for Edith's funeral in January 1981. Graham, who was then ninety-nine years old, but still completely clear in his mind, missed her terribly and for a short while we thought he would join her, but he rallied round and I think the prospect of reaching his century rather pleased him.

During the spring of 1981, when he spent much time reminiscing, Graham showed me the large collection of memorial cards they had kept over the years and explained who they were all referring to. Another source of information was the three old family bibles, two of which had lists of names and birth dates in them. Graham could remember so many of them, including his grandfather Humphrey Porter who was born in 1798 and died in 1889. Sadly he couldn't remember much about his mother Mary Jane, who died in 1885 aged forty-one, when Graham was only three, but he did have a sense of kindness and happiness about her. It appears that she was hardly ever mentioned after her death and the same thing happened in the next generation after the sudden death of Graham's brother's wife.

I have always been interested in the relationships in the family and over the years I had gathered a great deal of information in my head but had never written it down. Now was the time to start doing so, and I soon had a list of over 200 names, many of whom were living, of course, and included Graham and Edith's 27 grandchildren and, at that time, 35 great-grandchildren. (There are now 56, plus four great-greats.)

To go further back in the family history I had to look at Church records, but before that our daughter Claire and I had a day touring the relevant part of the Cotswolds. She was learning to drive at the time, so we set off early one July morning and she had a valuable 170 miles driving practice that day. We had with us a list of the places we wished to visit, all mentioned on the memorial cards or family bibles: Poulton, Southrop, Great and Little Barrington, Windrush, Sherborne, Clapton, Wyck Rissington, Icomb, Bourton-on-the-Water, Lyneham, Fulbrook, Burford and Holwell. This trip brought the places to life, of course. For instance, we could see where Graham's father, Thomas West Porter, was baptised in Southrop in 1844, where he was married in Great Barrington in 1871 and where he was buried in Burford in 1917.

There was no point in going to St Catherine's House in London where the births, marriages and deaths records are kept as they only begin in 1837 and I had already gone beyond that date from family records. Graham's sister, Lizzie, had drafted a rough family tree going back to their grandfather Humphrey, and on it she had written what Graham had mentioned: that one of the ancestors had had 26 children. I know that large families are a Porter feature (I won't say failing), but this did seem a bit excessive.

So the next step was to visit the County Records Office in Gloucester where most of the relevant Church registers are now stored. The staff there were most helpful (and still are), as also was Mr Brian Frith and I would like to thank them all for their patient assistance. I knew from the memorial cards and bible entries which parishes to look at (all villages in the Cotswolds) and I soon found that all the ancestors were from farming families: the sons married local farmers' daughters and the daughters married local farmers' sons. It was in the Eastleach Turville records that I discovered that it was Graham's great-great-grandfather Humphry who was the father of 26 children – by three wives I hasten to add.

I had paid four visits to Gloucester Record Office by the end of August when we held a big party to celebrate Graham's 100th birthday. By then there were 300 names on the family tree which I wrote out on a roll of wall paper. I had found that Humphry, father of 26, was the grandson of John Porter who was buried in Sherborne in 1700. The problem was to find out where he was born.

In the autumn of 1981 I went to a series of evening classes on genealogy which were useful, but I didn't do any more research at that time. For Christmas I was given *The Family History Book, A Guide to Tracing your Ancestors* by Stella Colwell, published by Phaidon Press, Oxford, which is a helpful book in many ways, including some hints on deciphering old writing which can be very difficult to understand. In the spring of 1982 my father-in-law started to show me some old account books, diaries, notes and letters, bringing out one or two each time I visited him. He loved to look over the old photographs and point out who was who.

All this whetted my appetite to try to find out more so I obtained a reader's ticket for the Bodleian Library in Oxford and looked up references to Endymion Porter, groom of the bedchamber to Charles I, as it appeared there could be a connection. I paid two or three more visits to Gloucester, looking up wills and any other relevant information. I wrote to the Royal College of Heralds who, for the sum of £65, looked up the records and found that this family of Porters does not have the right to bear the Porter arms which are: sable, three church bells argent, that is: black with three large, silver bells.

David and I stayed in the Cotswolds in the autumn of 1982 and visited all the places connected with the family, including Mickleton where we found that a board above the church door refers to Richard Porter starting a trust in 1512 for the benefit of the church and the poor of the parish. At the beginning of February Graham revealed the last of the family memorabilia and only a week later he had a heart attack. He was ill for just one month and died peacefully on 7th March 1983 aged 101.

Soon after that I started to put all the information together. I did visit St Catherine's House, London, after all, as I wanted to find out what was written on some of the death certificates. I also visited Somerset House to see what wills I could find, but I had obtained most of the details from Gloucester Record Office. Just recently David has helped me to collect census details from Gloucester and Oxford Libraries, and I was also very pleased to find in the Gloucester Record Office the inventory made at the time of John Porter's death in 1700. A combination of events seemed to hinder me from doing any more about putting the information together until this year when I was urged to do something about it by David and the family.

I had already met Mrs June O'Carroll Robertson who had her family history, *A Long Way From Tipperary*, published by Images in 1993, and I am most grateful for her advice and for introducing me to Images who immediately showed an interest in *Yeomen of the Cotswolds*. They introduced me to Mary Abbott who has brought her wide and expert historical knowledge to the book. I would like to thank Mary, as well as Tony Harold and Catherine Whiting from Images and also Andrew Best for all their help, advice and encouragement.

I owe a debt of gratitude to David's cousin Arthur Porter for finding, in the Museum of Naive Art in Bath, the copy of the painting reproduced on the dust jacket. This picture is now owned by Iona Antiques and I am grateful to them for allowing it to be used. It belonged to the family at one time and depicts William Lane, who was Arthur and David's great-great uncle. His prize-winning sheep were the subject of another painting and I am grateful to David's brother Basil for allowing this to be reproduced; and further thanks to Arthur for allowing a copy of the portrait of William Lane's mother Jane to be included in the book. Thanks must also go to the Centre for Oxfordshire Studies, Central Library, Westgate, Oxford, for allowing two of their archive photographs of Burford High Street to be included in the book.

I was glad that David's brothers Frank and Alan, as well as Arthur, were able to read my original manuscript and check on the accuracy of the farming and family facts and I thank them and all my brothers- and sisters-in-law and other family and friends for their interest and encouragement. My thanks must also go to my daughter Claire and sons Graham, Cedric and Jonathan who have heard about this project (on and off) for more than ten years and have always shown an interest. But the biggest thank you must be to David without whom this book would never have seen the light of day. For all his help, encouragement, interest and support I am most sincerely grateful and would like to dedicate *Yeomen of the Cotswolds* to him.

Eleanor Porter
Penton Grafton, December 1994.

The Porter family in June 1994. Most of Graham and Edith Porter's offspring (plus partners) – 27 grandchildren, 56 great-grandchildren and 4 great-great grandchildren. Only a dozen of these are engaged in farming. Among the rest are university lecturers, teachers, doctors, nurses, accountants and business managers.

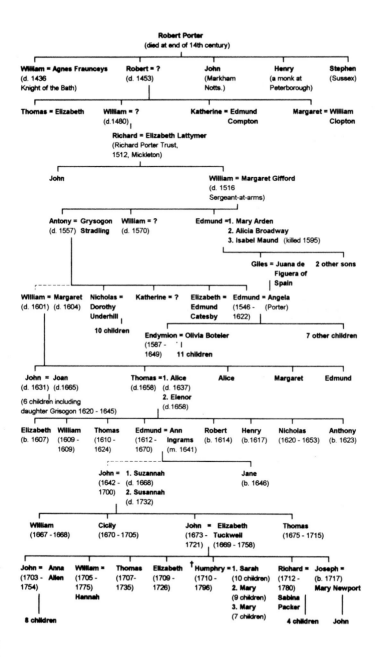

16

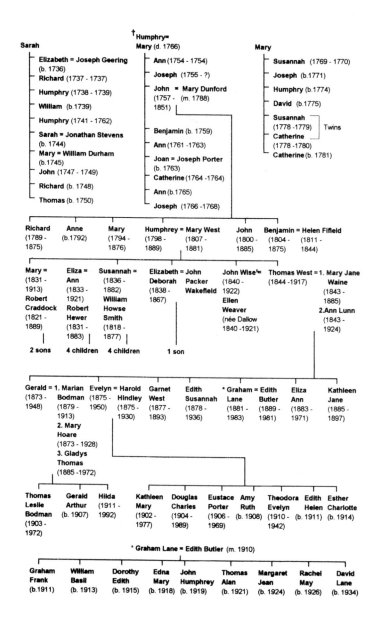

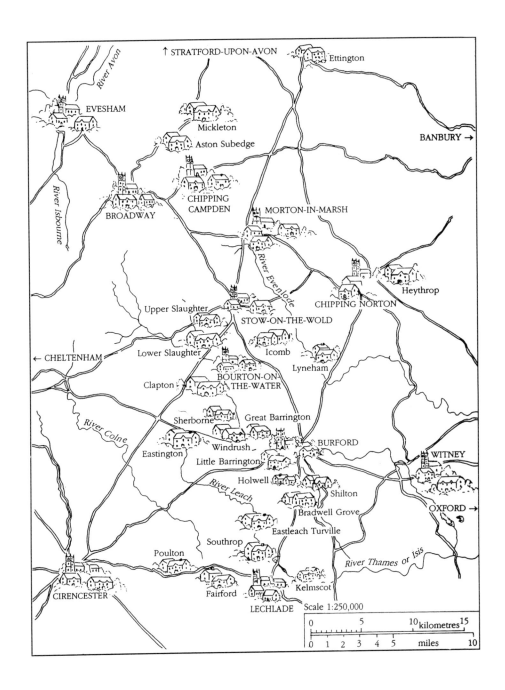

↑ STRATFORD-UPON-AVON
Ettington
River Avon
EVESHAM
Mickleton
Aston Subedge
BANBURY →
River Isbourne
CHIPPING CAMPDEN
MORTON-IN-MARSH
BROADWAY
River Evenlode
Heythrop
Upper Slaughter
CHIPPING NORTON
STOW-ON-THE-WOLD
Icomb
← CHELTENHAM
Lower Slaughter
Lyneham
Clapton
BOURTON-ON-THE-WATER
River Colne
Sherborne
Great Barrington
Eastington
Windrush
BURFORD
WITNEY
Little Barrington
Holwell
River Leach
Shilton
OXFORD →
Bradwell Grove
Eastleach Turville
Southrop
Poulton
River Thames or Isis
CIRENCESTER
Fairford
Kelmscot
LECHLADE

Scale 1:250,000

0   5   10 kilometres 15

0 1 2 3 4 5   miles   10

Introduction

oday, visitors are drawn to the Cotswolds by the harmony of landscape and buildings and by a curious feeling that they are travelling back into the past. When Algernon Gissing 'made acquaintance' with 'this quiet corner' in the 1880s he felt he was 'stepping back into Elizabethan England', almost onto the set of a Shakespearean production. No doubt he was thinking of *As You Like It* and the old Shepherd Corin, 'the natural philosopher' who knew that 'good pasture makes fat sheep . . .'

Cotswold churches, houses, barns and boundary walls seem to spring naturally from the landscape. Aptly so, for the towns and villages are built from the same stone on which they stand: the story goes that at Little Barrington the landlady of the New Inn used to call the quarrymen to their dinner by knocking on the floor.

The Cotswolds extend across five ancient shires. Gloucester has the lion's share, then Oxford, but Warwickshire (Shakespeare's county), Wiltshire and Worcestershire also include Cotswold acres. They are a span of the 'golden band' of Jurassic limestone which girds England from the Wash to the 'bone museum' of fossils on the coast of Dorset.

For centuries the area yielded harvests of stone, sheep and corn. The stone is easily worked, durable and handsome; it found favour with the builders of Oxford colleges and of the great palace built outside Woodstock for the first Duke of Marlborough, victor of Blenheim. The husbandry and sales of corn and sheep gave a rhythm and routine to the waking lives of Cotswold yeomen.

The yeomen of the eastern Cotswolds, whose story this book tells, were tenant farmers for three hundred years or more, moving from farm to farm within an easy ride or walk of the market town of Burford. It was at Burford that the annual hiring fair was held: there, in the autumn, at the turn of the farming year, the Porters and their kinsmen took on the shepherds, the ploughmen and the other men, boys and maids who formed the regular workforce of their farms. Unlike the country landowners, our yeomen did not practise primogeniture, which endows the eldest son at the expense of his younger brothers. Rather, they invested their wealth in making heirs of all their children, setting their sons up as farmers on their own account as they came to maturity, usually within a few miles of the house in which they were born. Their daughters' portions went to stock their husbands' farms.

The beauty of the Cotswolds has long been recognised; indeed, the region was the conservators' first battleground. It was the Victorian taste and stubbornness of Mr Cass, vicar of Burford, which provoked the writer and designer William Morris to establish the Society for the Protection of Ancient Buildings. Riled by Morris's trenchant criticism of the unsympathetic and unhistorical work done on Burford Church in the 1870s, Cass replied: 'The Church is mine and, if I choose, I shall stand on my head in it. '

It was because Burford combined 'domesticity' with 'romance', because it appeared to be a 'slumberous . . . ancient entity' that, from the first years of the twentieth century, the town attracted so many writers, painters and the painstaking, if sometimes misguided, restorers of ancient houses.

The process of elevating the Cotswolds to the status of a national treasure was under way by the 1870s when William Morris took the lease of Kelmscott Manor, which was to become his family's country home. He died in 1896 at Kelmscott House in Hammersmith and was buried in the churchyard at Kelmscott in Oxfordshire. The account of his final journey, printed in the *Saturday Review*, added a dimension to the image of an idealised rural way of life which he had done so much to promote among the English middle classes. A train carried the coffin, 'a very plain box', to Lechlade Station where it was transferred to a horse-drawn cart.

> No red-faced men in shabby black to stagger with the coffin to the hearse but in their place four countrymen in moleskin bore the body to an open haycart festooned with vines, with alder and with bullrushes and driven by a man who looked coeval with the Anglo-Saxon Chronicle.

In the late nineteenth century the Cotswolds were colonised by Morris's disciples, designer-craftsmen in revolt against the mass-produced, and dedicated to traditional ways of working wood and metal. In 1902 C. R. Ashbee transplanted his Guild of Handicraft from the Mile End Road in the East End of London to Chipping Campden in the Cotswolds. Cabinet makers and carvers, jewellers, silversmiths, enamellers and printers were installed in the Old Silk Mill in Sheep Street.

It was about this time too that Frederick Griggs, the artist who was to devote much of his life to recording the beauties of the Cotswolds' landscape and buildings, first got to know the area well while preparing the illustrations for the volume covering the Cotswolds in Macmillan's popular series of guidebooks to England's *Highways and Byways*. H. A. Evans, who wrote the text, conceived it as a blueprint for 'a summer excursion into the hill country' north-west of

Oxford. Like earlier guides he viewed the Cotswolds as 'an old-world English countryside', unfriendly to the bicycle, his chosen mode of transport, since the byways were rendered 'hopelessly sticky and impassable' by even a few hours' rain.

The colonisation of Burford by the artistic classes was chronicled by Mary Sturge Gretton in *Burford Past and Present*[1]. The work of writers and artists who settled there helped to spread Burford's reputation.

Burford High Street, looking down the hill, early twentieth century, courtesy of Westgate Library, Oxford.

[1] First published by Faber in 1920 and revised and expanded in 1929 and 1944.

Burford High Street, looking down the hill, late twentieth century.

By the time that J. B. Priestley made his English Journey in 1933 the Cotswolds had established themselves as 'the most English and least spoiled of all our countrysides . . . a national heritage of great value' which, 'so far as it is possible, should be acquired by the nation itself.' Driving through the Cotswolds on an autumn morning, 'one moved through a world of wet gold', and 'even when the sun is obscured and the light is cold' Cotswold walls 'are still faintly warm and luminous, as if they knew the trick of keeping the warm sunlight of centuries glimmering about them. This lovely trick is at the very heart of the Cotswold mystery . . . not a sunny morning since the Wars of the Roses has passed here without conjuring a little of its golden warmth into these stones.'

Priestley recognised the danger of over-exposure, but tourism was also to provide an alternative to the shrinking employment opportunities on the land. Sydney Bolton Russell was perhaps the first businessman to spot and exploit the Cotswolds' dual potential as a tourist trap and mecca for antique collectors. Having tried and failed to persuade his employers, a firm of Burton brewers, to develop the Lygon Arms at Broadway as a country hotel, Russell raised the funds to buy this 'splendid piece of Cotswold architecture' himself. He set out to recreate an 'Old English Hostelry', hung with Flemish tapestries and furnished with old pieces of oak which had been restored by his own team of craftsmen. He opened an antique shop nearby and stocked it with items surplus to the hotel's requirements. Among the shop's customers was Henry Ford, who bought exhibits for his museum in Detroit, including the contents of a local blacksmith's shop.

Russell brought up his sons to carry on the family trade. Don ran the hotel until his death in the 1970s. Gordon was put in charge of the restoration workshop and became known as a designer of 'decent furniture for ordinary people', the man who harnessed the power of machinery to make affordable chairs and tables in the style of Morris and Ashbee. During the Second World War he led the team which produced designs for the elegant but functional Utility furniture made to equip the homes of newly-married couples and families which had been 'bombed out'.

In virtually every parish in which the Porter family lived and worked, the riches of carving or architecture merit a detour: the Dutton monuments at Sherborne, the twin churches and the clapper bridge which links them at Eastleach, the font at Southrop which depicts the virtues victorious over vice. Each virtue triumphs over its vicious opposite: pity over envy; temperance over luxury; generosity over avarice; patience over anger; modesty over excess. The vices' retreat is symbolised by the inversion of their mirror-carved Latin names.

Temperance and modesty were the virtues of which yeomen were particularly proud.

Though men of substance – 'chief farmers', they were referred to in one seventeenth century document – yeomen were distinct from the squirearchy in three principal ways: they were more often tenants than owners of land; their way of life was more frugal, less showy; and the world which they inhabited was smaller, bounded by the market town, the hiring fair at which they recruited their workers, and the sales at which they disposed of their livestock. They were practical farmers, and their wives, with few maids to assist them, were practical housekeepers, delegating the roughest work but supervising and participating in the daily tasks of the kitchen, the poultry yard and the dairy. The stiff poses of studio portraits, the *cartes de visites* which provide us with images of whole generations of Cotswold yeomen and their families from the 1860s and 1870s, display men and women at their most formal. The women are seen as ladies of leisure but a moment's consideration of the large households they managed with a single live-in maid makes it likely that a Victorian Mrs Porter would invariably be wearing her pinafore. Since 'waste not, want not' was their maxim, we may assume that, stripped of its trimmings, 'old best' was eventually relegated to workaday wear. Stout garments had long lives, as a letter from William Butler to his granddaughter Edith Porter in December 1919 makes clear. He wrote: 'I thank you very much for the Waistcoat and Letter, and so kind of you thinking about me. The Vest fits me nicely over a Wool knitted one which I had in the year 1852.'

The richer yeomen of the sixteenth and earlier seventeenth centuries were 'gentlemen in ore'; quite often the farm profit would fund an eldest son's promotion to the ranks of the landed gentry. Many of those who sent their sons to university founded dynasties of parsons. Our line of Cotswold yeomen achieved its status too late to aspire to the manor house or parsonage, but ingrained habits of diligence and thrift equipped them to endure lean years and put something by when times were better. As Nathaniel Newbury put it in a sermon written for the yeomen of Kent in 1652 –

> Consider that thou sowest thy furrow by the handful, not by the sack . . . Be frugal while you have it; it will be too late to put two fingersful in the purse when you have thrown all away by handfuls.

Modest luxuries were not excluded by this code – indeed small indulgences protected a family against charges of parsimony. In the Porter family, silver tankards and spoons were the eighteenth century tokens; in the nineteenth century, flower gardens, summer houses and Wedgwood dinner services; and in the twentieth century, motor cars. By this time, it would be fair to describe them as a playwright had described a Kentish yeoman three centuries earlier: 'half farmer, and half gentleman'. His horses went 'to the plough all week, and are put into the coach o' Sunday'.

To our way of thinking the houses which yeomen occupied in the nineteenth century are not only handsome but rather grand. We tend to forget that, as families have shrunk from many children to a few and as domestic technology has replaced domestic servants, houses have, in a way, gone up in the world.

The parish churches where they worshipped, on the other hand, though often well preserved, may be said to have come down in the world, with congregations pitifully reduced; but for our yeomen they were the time-honoured setting for life's great ceremonies – baptism, marriage, and the funeral which came to its solemn close with burial in the church itself or the churchyard. There is a stone in the church at Eastleach Turville, now partly masked by a step, which commemorates John Porter, who died on 29 March 1721, and his wife Elizabeth, who survived him by thirty-seven years. Before the middle of the nineteenth century few other members of the family left such a monument in church or churchyard.

Our yeomen of the Cotswolds include devout men and women who rejected the physical glories of their parish churches and opted to worship elsewhere, urged on by the dictates of conscience. In the 1820s Thomas West of Icomb in Gloucestershire left the Church of England to become a Baptist. In the 1880s his nephew and namesake Thomas West Porter rejected the Anglican Church to become a member of the Exclusive Brethren.

For farmers, the Cotswolds was and is a working landscape. To them the lie of the land was not important in terms of its aesthetic qualities, but simply for its farming potential, founded in the complementary production of sheep and corn. The notion of a holiday away from home came late to the farming community: whilst landlords had travelled in pursuit of health and entertainment since the seventeenth century, a Porter yeoman did not venture afield until the nineteenth, and did so then to convalesce, in accordance with the wisdom of his time, on the bracing Sussex Coast. When Thomas West Porter took his bride on honeymoon it was to the Isle of Wight and the couple brought back news of Shanklin Chine and the royal retreat at Osborne. One wonders what the Victorian farmer would have made of the tourists who descend in ever-increasing numbers upon the villages and countryside of the Cotswolds most days of the year.

We have adopted what might be termed an archaeological approach to the history of our yeomen of the Cotswolds, investigating their experience stratum by stratum, starting with the, perhaps rather rose-tinted, memoirs of a member of the last generation of Cotswold farmers and working back; in fact this approach mirrors the process of discovery as the Porter family archives and public records were excavated layer by layer. Understandably the recent past is in sharpest focus; as we track back in time the material at our disposal becomes more sparse. This decline in the volume and richness of the documentary evidence occurs not at a steady rate but unevenly: thus we have better data for the eighteenth than for the first part of the nineteenth century. However, until we reach the mid-sixteen hundreds, there is no single weak or debatable link in the chain.

Naturally, a word-of-mouth version of the history of our yeomen circulated in the Porter family before any research was carried out, and it seems only fair to put our readers on a similar footing.

The first members of the Porter family whom we can identify with confidence are William, whose baptism was registered at Sherborne in Gloucestershire in 1667, and his parents, John and Susannah. We are not certain where they came from. A search through entries in the surviving parish registers of Gloucestershire and Oxfordshire produced two candidates: John Porter born at Ashleworth, Oxfordshire, about twenty-five miles from Sherborne, in 1637; and John Porter, born at Mickleton in the north of Gloucestershire, slightly closer to Sherborne, in 1642. None of the given names which recur in the family recorded in the Ashleworth registers was passed down the generations to the descendants of John Porter of Sherborne, whereas some of those at Mickleton were. The Mickleton registers provide us with the names of John Porter's parents, grandparents and great-grandparents: William, who was buried in 1602, and Margaret, his wife, who was buried two years later. William's date and place of birth are uncertain. One superficially, but ultimately unconvincing, hypothesis, explained more fully in chapter 15, identified William with a branch of the Porter family that can be traced back to Robert Porter, who died at Ettington in the fourteen century.

It was usual, then as now, for newly married couples to set up homes of their own and, although it may be natural to assume that, in a horse-powered era, men and women married their next door neighbours and settled close to their parents, the considerable evidence at our disposal suggests that this was not the case. In the seventeenth century the sons of modest farmers frequently spent their youth as servants in husbandry, resident farm workers. By custom, they moved from farm to farm in late September – Michaelmas, which marked the end of the harvest year – accumulating the knowledge that they would deploy when, in due course, if all went well, they set up as farmers on their own account. These frequent moves, albeit within the orbit of a single market town, complicate the task of the family historian seeking to identify her subjects' parentage and place of birth.

Baby William and his mother Susannah were buried at Sherborne in 1668. John, whom we call John Porter I to distinguish him from descendants with the same given name, soon remarried. As the singing game puts it, 'The farmer needs a wife' to take responsibility for the women's side of the traditional farming enterprise – the household, the dairy and the hens. John's second marriage was longer lasting and more fruitful. Three children were baptised: Cicily in 1670, John in 1673 and Thomas in 1675. Our line of the Porter family descends from John Porter II who settled in Eastleach Turville, a few miles from his birthplace. Like other tenant farmers, successive generations of the

Porter family shifted from holding to holding in search of more favourable terms or better land. Sons who came of age while their fathers were in their prime took on farms of their own in the neighbourhood, often with financial assistance from their fathers.

John Porter II died young for a Porter, still under fifty. Humphry (1710-1796), the fourth of his six sons, moved from Eastleach Turville to Southrop. He and his three fertile wives brought infants to the font over a remarkably long period. For our purposes, the most significant child of this generation was John – John Porter III – (1757-1851), who farmed at Great Barrington. His son Humphrey (1798-1889), also of Great Barrington, was the father of Thomas West Porter who moved a couple of miles across the county boundary from Gloucestershire to Oxfordshire to take up the tenancy of Manor Farm in Holwell in 1870. His decision to leave the Church of England and join the Exclusive Brethren was to have a profound effect on later generations of his family.

Thomas West Porter's sons, Gerald (1873-1948) and Graham (1881-1983), were the last of the family to farm in the Cotswolds, Gerald farmed there until his retirement; Graham ended his farming career in Hampshire, where his son David and David's wife Eleanor now live.

The Porter family archives are rich and this, therefore, is an account of a dynasty of Cotswold yeomen, given, as far as possible, in their own words . . .

Part One

RELIVING THE PAST

Chapter One

MANOR FARM

uch of the material for the next four chapters is taken from only two sources: Gerald Porter's memoir *Plum Money*, which he wrote at the age of seventy, in 1943, and brought up to date shortly before his death in 1948; and the reminiscences which Graham Lane Porter put down on paper in 1981, when he was one hundred years old. Other family papers embody the reflections of yeomen of the Cotswolds in old age – wills and the overview of farming in Oxfordshire which Thomas West Porter, father of Gerald and Graham, wrote at the end of his long career are examples. Change is an essential feature of these reflections but so is a sense of continuity. In wills, in particular, the focus is on handing on: not only the handing on of capital and personal possessions but also of responsibilities and especially of responsibility for those who, for one reason or another, could not care for themselves. Gerald Porter and his younger brother Graham were the first members of their family who felt a need to leave a detailed record of their way of life. In no other generation was there a sense that members of this farming family had spent their childhood in what would be, to their descendants, a strange country in which one's own grandchildren would be disorientated, unable to find their way without a guide.

The sensation of loss was not peculiar to the Porter family. *Plum Money* is an example of what H. J. Massingham, author of *Shepherd's Country*, called 'memorial books', written to record a passing, or past, way of life in the English countryside. The designer and gardener Gertrude Jekyll, a Surrey gentlewoman born in 1843, who published *Old West Surrey* in 1904, and the wheelwright George Sturt, born in 1863, author of the classic *The Wheelwright's Shop*, were pioneers of the genre to which Gerald's near contemporaries, Walter Rose, born in 1871, and Flora Thompson, born in 1877, were notable contributors.

Prompted by a widespread feeling that the traditional ways of living and working were being swept away, and the evidence of the public's appetite, which had been stimulated by the success of earlier publications, a cluster of 'memorial books' came out around the time that Gerald wrote *Plum Money*. Flora Thompson's *Lark Rise to Candleford* was published in 1939 and Walter Rose's *Good Neighbours – Recollections of an English Village and its People* appeared in 1942. War increased the recorders' sense of urgency.

In the preface to *Good Neighbours*, Walter Rose describes his reasons for writing, reasons which Gerald Porter might well have endorsed:

> A man who knows the history of his village has . . . a sense of responsibility; he realizes that his unique information ought to be shared with other people, and he feels obliged to put it on record.

Born two years before Gerald, Walter Rose was

> . . . inclined to regard the year 1871 as a fortunate date for my birth; it was early enough for me to catch the fag end

of the old order of life that, even then, was rapidly passing: and late enough for me to witness the change over to conditions still prevailing today. Hence I can claim to belong to both old and new; and, whereas little purpose would be served in describing what everyone today can see for themselves, the life of my early years has already become interesting and strange.

H. J. Massingham saw his family history as that of many hundreds of thousands of English countrymen, 'from the village craftsman or land-labourer to the estate owner who were compelled to leave a pauperised countryside in order to become businessmen or factory-hands or clerks or journalists or artists or officials or dole-men in London', and thus became a dedicated recorder of the traditions of rural life which slipped away during the first half of Graham Lane Porter's lifetime. When he made his pilgrimage to the *Shepherd's Country* of the Cotswolds in the 1930s Massingham came across Farmer Garne of Aldsworth, a kinsman of the Porters, and his old shepherd Wilcox who kept the last commercial flock of the native Cotswold sheep in the world. Mrs Garne showed Massingham two large paintings of the early nineteenth century wherein the rams were as big as bullocks, chesty to extravagance and bare along their heads, necks and legs.

> Nowadays [he observed] the wool is let to grow right up to the eyes with the great forelock or lovelock reaching almost to the nose . . . A leg of mutton from these sheep weighs between thirty and forty pounds, and this badge of their magnificence (what an inn-sign!) has been the

reason for their undoing . . . Farmer Garne maintains the immemorial breed as much for honour's sake as for profit . . .

They are extremely long in the leg and broad in the beam and muscles of their chests ripple as they move. Teats are full and round, ears long and tapering, and the space between them curly as Ganymede's hair . . . The fleeces are curly throughout and tend to make a parting down the back. The face, too, is long, the look proud, the movement both slow and deliberate, and the feet are lifted well off the ground. It is a walk stately, unhurried, heavy in the tread . . . The chewing is much slower, the plucking of the grasses more leisurely and the jerk upwards of the head less abrupt and angular than among plebeian sheep.

Massingham watched the young rams as they were arrayed in what he calls 'their surcoats of orange-gold', the characteristic dressing of the Cotswold fleece. They 'properly' resented being watered with a can

. . . as though they were lobelias in a suburban garden, flinching, tossing their heads, shaking themselves spaniel-wise and even rearing up and beating the air with their forelegs. But through wind to the stars! and when they emerge from the ordeal . . . their fleeces match the ripening corn on the Aldsworth Downs. With my own eyes I have seen the golden fleece. The process is nothing but an ornamental heritage: it confers no benefit upon the sheep but merely glorifies them and drapes them with the beams of the sun. Or in Wilcox's more salty term: 'It makes 'em tuppy' – ready for the ewe. Both he and kindly Mr Garne insisted that the Cotswold rams were ochred for no better reason than carters plait and beribbon the manes and tails of their shire horses and because they have so tyred[2] them against the marriage day.

Massingham's high-flown prose was designed to appeal to those lobelia-growing suburbanites who explored the countryside in their motor cars and daydreamed about retiring to a cottage with roses growing round the door.

Gerald and Graham Lane Porter wrote primarily for their family. Gerald had a powerful historical imagination. In 1943 he set down an account of his childhood home, Manor Farm, at Holwell, the farm his brother Graham gave up in 1921. He took the story back, far beyond his father's arrival at Holwell in 1871, to the reign of 'the bigoted and soured' queen, 'Bloody Mary'. He pictured the first occupants of the house, overcoming their fear of night visitors to succour a 'weary and travel stained stranger' – William Tyndale, the Gloucestershire-born translator of the New Testament, who shared with them the gospel message 'in the simple English then spoken'. It was apt that Gerald should call up the martyred ghost who made the Bible 'such a homely thing'.

Gerald imagined the night in 1666 when the household at Holwell was aroused at midnight by a reddish light in the east which 'increased then lessened', unlike the familiar 'glowing heralding sunrise'. Days later the news came that 'a great part of the capital was burnt'. Then

---

[2] Attired.

there was the 'dull November day' in 1688 when the 'sound of horses approaching from the Burford direction' at 'the steady clatter of a jog-trot' signalled the arrival of a detachment of soldiers on their way to meet William of Orange. These episodes from the imagined past are shot through with reminders of the religious faith which shaped the family's history and of the war which was being waged as he wrote: the Great Fire brought to mind daylight saving and the more recent days when 'the sky over London was again . . . illuminated; this time as a result of the awful German blitz'.

Gerald Porter grew up at the time of the Great Agricultural Depression, when farmers' incomes, his father's included, slumped, yet *Plum Money* conveys very little of the anxieties which beset his father Thomas and his father's neighbours. As a young child, Gerald may have been shielded from the economic realities; and by the time he reached his teens and his own labour was invested in the farm, reductions in rent had done something to ease the lot of tenant farmers like his father. As well as this, the circumstances in which he wrote in the early 1940s, when the outcome of the war against Hitler remained in doubt, may have encouraged him to play down the economic hardships of his childhood.

In *Plum Money* Gerald Porter takes his readers on a guided tour of Manor Farm, Holwell, one of the seven farms on the Bradwell Grove Estate which was owned for fifty years from 1871 by William Henry Fox Esq. As Gerald noted, Holwell 'was on the extreme east of the Wolds, lacking one feature that adds charm to such villages, the rippling of the sparkling stream'. The village 'was set on rising ground and protected from the cold north and east by a magnificent belt of tall elms', these have since disappeared, victims of Dutch elm disease.

Manor Farm, Holwell.

This Cotswold house, where Gerald and his two brothers and four sisters grew up, was the setting for a way of life which had vanished since their childhoods in the 1870s and 1880s. Appropriately, he leads us in the back way – the front had been smartened up with gardens and a carriage drive.

A large flagged courtyard adjoined the back of the old house, where stood the pump that supplied the necessary water, with a deep old stone trough and, incidentally, a stone drain quite near the well. There was, too, a large

39

Portugal laurel tree, providing sanctuary for the army of cats from dogs and boys. The kitchen window with mullions and small panes looked out on to this courtyard and there were one or two windows that had been stopped up, evidently when the window tax was put on[3]. There were gables and a massive pile of chimneys and the whole was weathered by the storms of centuries.

But to reach this back of the house the farmyard had to be entered by a gate between the stable and the granary and pass the back of the nag stable[4] and coach houses, where were situated the pig sties. Then a flight of stone steps leading to various lofts, including the spray loft[5]. Next was the 'pig vault' out of which was tipped a liquid, composed of the kitchen waste of the house (and many other ingredients to judge by the smell), and into this liquid was stirred the meal fed to the pigs, who ate it with the greatest relish – and we ate the pigs . . .

Then there was the lime house, which seemed to contain everything except lime, and where incidentally cats could easily be 'bagged'. A door out of this led into a dark and fearsome chamber called the 'potato' house into which no self-respecting frost would enter, nor would little boys who had heard stories of dungeons and 'bogeymen'.

---

[3] The tax was in force between 1695 and 1851 but historians of buildings are not persuaded that tax evasion explains every 'blind' window.

[4] The home of the horse which pulled a trap rather than a farm cart or a plough.

[5] A store for the hairpin-shaped hazel sticks, sprays or spars used in thatching.

The coal house followed, large enough to hold tons of this mineral, and then the 'roost' inhabited by the many cocks and hens – of sundry breeds or of none at all – and a species of insect not usually associated with what is said to be next to godliness[6] and, be it remembered, that only the wood house was between the chamber of horrors, and the house itself – indeed an upper door led from a loft in this wood house into a room that was designated the Nursery as the family began to come along.

This range of buildings was on your right. On your left were horse yards with warm thatched bowsins[7], and then the duck house, wisely sparred[8] in front, as such birds are somewhat smelly, and prefer to lay their eggs in the dirtiest quarter. Next a timber store adjoining the carpenter's shop, where Charles Buckingham was to be found in wet weather, and whom we young fry liked very much (he had thirteen of his own) and who would let us use his tools. A timber yard came next, and in it a very large and tall elm, supporting hundreds of poles, stood upright around it, waiting to be made into hurdles etc. There was a saw-pit too, which was used occasionally and one never envied the task or position of the <u>bottom</u> sawyer. Stacks of faggots too, and then the wash house, containing two large coppers, and not infrequently used as a butcher's shop; for the pigs killed for the house were hung up and dissected with great surgical skill by my

---

[6] Lice or cockroaches.

[7] Shelters.

[8] Slatted.

father, and casualty sheep were hung there and sold out at a cheap rate. They were dressed very neatly by the shepherd in one of the horse yards – I don't know why there . . .

At the back of this building was a large ashpit[9], which was cleared when full – no weekly scavenging in those days. But, it must be added, that many of these somewhat crude features were eliminated in my very early days, and conditions assumed a more sanitary aspect in these regions . . .

On the right was the carthorse stable and over [which] was the 'tallot' where the fodder was kept, the hay being passed direct into the cribs above the mangers. (How wonderful that in such a manger, the Lord of Glory should have found his first resting place on earth – 'the Babe lying in a manger', and this witnessed by shepherds, themselves fulfilling an important role in agriculture – faithful men with their flock).

A very large barn adjoined the stable. There was the midstay with a pair of large doors each end so that loaded waggons of sheaves could be drawn in and unloaded into the larger section – ready for thrashing by the flail, sheaf by sheaf in this midstay which had a wooden floor, and the grain then sifted and winnowed and bagged in the smaller end of the barn, the straw and fodder being fed to the stock (cattle and pigs) in adjoining yards, who, I have been told, did very well, as their food was fresh daily,

---

[9] Into which the privies may have been emptied.

and, if a little grain escaped the flail, it was not wasted – the pigs saw to that, and so did the barndoor fowl. Of course, these remarks apply more particularly to oats and barley, the wheat straw would be kept for thatching, and many farm buildings and houses were thatched then, and the straw was not so bruised as by the machines of later years, and hence more suitable and lasting.

I cannot, of course, remember flail thrashing except on a very small scale. We had two flails hanging up in the barn for years. I have attempted to use them, but it usually resulted in a resounding whack on the head and the effort being given up in disgust.

The thrashers worked in pairs and kept up a steady and regular thump, thump, on the floor, weeks and months on end during the winter . . . There was no delay for bad weather as the work was under cover once the corn was drawn into the barn. Ten racks made a load, and wheat, at any rate, was often sold by such a measure. The sacks were four bushels, to measure not to weight, and there was a real knack in filling the bushel as lightly as possible; it must not be touched, the corn was sacked with a 'strike' which was like a huge rolling pin, so 'good measure shaken together and running over' was spoken of by the Lord as the reward for liberality. A huge key unlocked the barn door being so made to prevent the barn robbing of earlier days . . .

On one side of the barn was a small lean-to shed occupied by an old gander and his concubines. He was a terror to us boys and girls, and many a time we have run for our lives with him flapping and hissing at our heels. I did sometimes have a pitched battle with him, armed with a stiff besom, but the honours were not always on my side. My mother was braver and would grasp him by the neck and, after swinging him round and round, would let him go sprawling down the yard, which was not at all to his ideas of gander dignity . . .

A modern range of horse yards [backed] onto the garden. They were not Cotswold in that the roofs were of blue slates, but not so hideous as the new stable made of locally made brick and covered with corrugated iron. Admittedly this stable was more airy and sanitary, and in some respects more convenient . . .

Farmyard, Holwell.

Brought up in Buckinghamshire, Walter Rose, a village carpenter, shared Gerald's dislike of iron roofs.

> Galvanised sheet iron for covering roofs first appeared when I was a boy, and I remember my father's interest in it as a cheap and effective covering. But we did not foresee how widely it would come to be used.
>
> The picturesque roofs of thatch were being less and less lasting; the straw damaged by the threshing machine would not stand the weather so long; and the thatchers' charges were going up at the same time. This, together with the dread of fire and the fact that insurance rates were double, had made thatch unpopular . . . Canal building brought us slate from Wales. When the GWR[10] was made, large tiles from Bridgwater in Somerset came along, and many barns were covered with these. They were never quite satisfactory; snow filtered between them, and the old roofs were so steep that the tiles were too easily dislodged by winds and used to slide to the ground. Galvanised iron had none of these disadvantages; yet its use was an irritation to the true craftsman. Our hands were accustomed to the responsive feel of wood. We did not like handling the harshness of galvanised iron, or the look of it afterwards. One of father's men would say: Even a wheel barrow would catch cold under it!

To return to Gerald's description. On Manor Farm, there were

---

[10] Great Western Railway.

. . . commodious barns – all in Cotswold style and roomy cattle yards, whose bowsins were thatched, warm and comfortable.

There was the ewe pen too, an important spot where the lambing took place. This was a large yard with the bowsin facing south and west . . . a small part of the bowsin was enclosed as a house for the shepherd who often spent hours there on cold wintry nights.

So now – a brief notice of the Manor House: It was approached by a path of old flagstones. The outbuildings . . . mostly backed on to this path, though the two coach houses and hay stable faced it . . . These back walls were covered with evergreen climbing shrubs which gave a very pleasing effect. In fact, around the gable and roof of the Spray Loft, there grew a very nice white rambler rose with clusters of pure white bloom – the Seven Sisters by name, to see which, at one time, Mrs Fox[11] would bring her visitors after church on the Sunday nearest the longest day. . .

The original part of the house was a continuation of this range of buildings. This part seemed very old, more so than that which stood at right angles and thus formed the present front of the house, and where the front door is placed, where a very old vine flourished. The side door gave access to this old section so we will enter thereby even if we have to explore the kitchen before the parlour. As we enter, the back kitchen is on the left of the little

---

[11] Squire' Fox's mother from Bradwell Grove.

entrance lobby, and a very interesting (I say not 'convenient' or 'modern') room it is. A pitchful of pea straw was laid by the back door where there was a step down. This was excellent for wiping one's dirty farm boots on entry and was renewed each week when the place was swilled down, the maids walking about in pattens during this operation.

Flora Thompson provides us with a vivid picture of pattens. In her village, at the opposite corner of Oxfordshire:

The women wore pattens over their shoes to go to the well or the pigsty. The patten consisted of a wooden sole with a leather toepiece raised about two inches from the ground on an iron ring. *Clack! Clack! Clack!* over the stones, and *Slush! Slush! Slush!* through the mud went the patten rings. You could not keep your movements secret, if you wore pattens to keep yourself dry shod.

A pair of pattens only cost ten pence and lasted four years. But the patten was doomed. Vicarage ladies and farmers' wives no longer wore them to go to and fro between their dairies and their poultry yards and newly married cottagers no longer provided themselves with a pair. 'Too proud to wear pattens' was already becoming a proverb at the beginning of the decade, and by the end of it they had practically disappeared.

Gerald's memoirs go on to describe the back kitchen at Manor Farm.

. . . immediately on our left, and under the window, is a huge washing-up stone trough; it was hollowed out of one large block of local freestone. The sides and bottom had become very irregular, the result of constant – perhaps of centuries' – use. It was modern enough to have a tap above supplying water and a vent hole to take this away, but this ran into a very antiquated and untrapped stone drain which traversed the length of the room and emptied outside not far from the well that supplied the house. Small wonder that bad throats were experienced and that drastic measures had to be taken to deal with such effluent.

A very old fashioned plate rack, with no draining board, stood next, and in the corner was the potato cupboard, large enough on occasions for young farm hands to hide in from my father's wrath when they came into the house 'sweethearting' the servant girls.

There were two coppers, one on each side of the large hearth from which proceeded a capacious chimney. It was large enough for a ladder to be put up and for a man (in a special smock) to ascend, taking sides of bacon which were hung there to be smoked. Old fashioned chimney irons hung out over the hearth on which pots and kettles were hung, and underneath was an oven with a small hearth under this so that it could be heated above and below. Only wood was used as a fuel, and this too was better for drying the bacon . . .

In another corner was the bread oven which I can remember my mother using on occasion. It was of course heated by being filled with faggot wood, and when all this burnt out, the ashes were quickly swept out with a long-handled kind of mop – I forget what it was called – and the bread etc. put in and left to bake, which it did beautifully, but it must have been a skilled job to get the right heat and to keep [the bread] free from ashes.

Bacon racks hung from the ceiling on which the flitches[12] were placed after smoking in the chimney. There was a small round ash table on three legs at which the servant-maid usually dined and which had evidently been used for a similar purpose for the men that at one time were provided with board and lodging in the farmhouse. This table had deep cuts in the edge and, I think, some initials were roughly carved on its surface. Of course, we took no account of such a piece of furniture, but it would be of value now . . .

. . . Now to the kitchen . . . This room was entered by turning right at the side door. It was very low, and two large beams traversed the ceiling . . . these inclined a little in the centre, no doubt having supported the floor above for centuries. I expect they were oak but [they] had been encased in lathe and plaster, which was a great pity. One went into the chimney, and, not surprisingly, caught fire on one occasion, mercifully with no serious result, and was then encased in iron.

The two windows, mullioned, were opposite each other. On one pane was cut a very old-fashioned 'W' . . .

---

[12] Sides of bacon.

The old people said that the last birth in the house, previous to my own, was that of a Wells, a hundred years before, and the place 'ought to belong to that there boy' [Gerald himself], which, however, it never has done or will do . . .

The floor of the kitchen was uneven flagstones, and there were four doors leading [from it] besides cupboard and dresser doors *ad lib*. We used it a good deal for meals, but it was a cold comfortless room, and the memory of half-past-six breakfasts on a wintry morning still sends a cold shiver down one's spine.

One of the four doors . . . led into a room that was divided by wooden partitions into pantries and the dairy. They were rather dark, as the chief window – mullioned – was more or less overgrown with ivy. I should think formerly this room had been the principal one in the old part of the house. There was a large fireplace which in our day had been enclosed and formed a capacious cupboard where the dry kindle wood was stored. These rooms . . . formed, I imagine, the original house, so before proceeding further on the ground floor, we will ascend the winding stairs from the kitchen and have a look at the bedrooms and attics above. Over the present pantries was the 'boys room' and a bitterly cold one it was. The only window was north and, of course, there was no heat from below. The floor sloped decidedly to one corner – still the boys survived this. On occasion the water in the jugs froze solid and split [them].

The girls' room was over the kitchen and, of course,

much warmer. It was wainscoted all round, really beautiful oak panelling but which, Victorian-like, had been painted over, and the west window had been blocked up and converted into a linen cupboard. This room had at first been our parents room and some of us older ones first saw the light therein. A lobby led into the room over the back kitchen, which became the nursery. There was in it a large old-fashioned box-mangle loaded with stones to furnish the necessary pressure, but the handle of this was (wisely) kept fastened up in case mangled fingers or bodies, should result.

From this first floor another winding stair led up to the two attics – one where the maids slept, and the other used as an apple store, with a door leading out onto the roof. They were eerie sorts of places and, the apple room especially, the resort of rats. And why apples should have been carried up two flights of crooked stairs which had to be climbed every time any were wanted for cooking, was a bit of a mystery, though, be it remembered, in such a place they were comparatively safe from the depredations of boys – for 'boys will be boys' and 'apples, apples' too.

I believe in a winter's gale some of the attic window panes were broken when a large elm tree broke and crashed that way – the stump is still there – so that sometimes these attics must have been rather nerve-racking for the maids, but I suppose they worked hard and slept soundly.

Some of the maids served long years at Manor Farm. Gerald quoted an entry from one of his father's lists of Michaelmas hirings, now lost: 'Hired Lydia Brunsdon 1876/77. £3.00 and if a good girl promised her a new dress.' With benefit of long hindsight, he added:

> As she stayed for 33 years, presumably she got the new dress and eventually her wages rose to the munificent amount of £13 10s 0d per annum and she had a legacy under her mistress's will, as well she might for she was a faithful servant.

Gerald described the rest of the house only briefly: dining room, spacious hall, drawing room, and more bedrooms. Graham's reminiscences, though briefer than his brother's, confirm Gerald's description. Graham's distinctive contribution reflects his fascination with the technical. He dwells, characteristically, on the difference in domestic technology between Manor Farm in the 1880s and the 'all-electric' houses with which his grandchildren were familiar. At Manor Farm there was

> . . . no electricity for lighting the house this being done either by candles or paraffin lamps which needed refilling with oil and trimming once a week, a dirty and tedious job.
>
> The cellar – underneath the drawing room . . . was . . . cooler in summer than the rest of the house so it took the place in some degree of the present-day refrigerators.

Having set the scene, Gerald Porter introduces his readers to the most colourful member of the cast of farmworkers, the Shepherd.

Chapter Two

THE COTSWOLD SHEPHERD

t was fitting that, in his memorial portrait of a Cotswold farm, Gerald Porter should give the shepherd and his calendar pride of place.

Cotswold shepherds were not peculiar in being, as Gerald put it, 'a law unto themselves'. In his autobiographical novel, *Farmer's Glory*, published in 1932 and set discreetly 'in southern England', Arthur Street referred to 'the autocracy of shepherds'.

John Winfield was Shepherd at Manor Farm for nearly half a century. Thomas West Porter took him on the year after he moved to Manor Farm to replace Vincent Matthews the shepherd whom he had inherited with the tenancy – at seventy-seven the old man had come to the end of his working life, but he stayed on in the shepherd's cottage until he died. Graham Porter, who took Manor Farm on when his father retired in 1910, remembered Shepherd Winfield well: 'he was a very faithful and honest servant, . . . being rightly termed a good shepherd and whilst with us he got to know the Good Shepherd and bore a bright testimony to Him'. It was John Winfield's misfortune to preside over his flock in the declining years of the Cotswold sheep's popularity.

Shepherd and master encountered each other for the first time on 25 September 1872 – at Burford Hiring Fair. As Gerald Porter recalled, the men looking for places wore tokens of their trade on their hats: 'shepherds – a tuft of wool; carters – whipcords; grooms a sponge; cowmen – end of cow's tail; engine drivers – a grimy face and blue smock'. 'If', to quote Graham Lane Porter, 'the job appealed to the man and the man to the master, they discussed and settled their terms and wages, and made a contract to last a year, the master giving the man one shilling, termed earnest money, which was supposed to clinch the contract.'

Burford Hiring Fair, c. 1895, courtesy of Westgate Library, Oxford.

According to his father's note of the men he took on at Michaelmas 1874, Shepherd Winfield was hired at

> . . . two shillings a week more than daymen[13], £2 for lambing and three shillings a score for shearing, two bushels of malt for haymaking, two bushels for harvest, one pig at a shilling a score less than market price and cottage free.

On 11 October 1872, a waggon and a cart were despatched from Manor Farm to bring John Winfield, his wife Eliza and little boy William and all their goods and chattels to a tiny cottage carved out of the end of a barn. When the old shepherd died not too long after, the Winfields moved into the cottage which traditionally went with the job. And, in due course, their baby son acquired nine brothers and sisters. Gerald recalled that:

> Shepherd[14] [Winfield] was of medium height, spare and wiry, a fringe of whiskers round his shaven face, very spray-footed and walked much on his heels.
>
> . . . [He was] an intelligent man and very well spoken. He developed a curious habit when discussing matters with my father; . . . standing with his back to him, and thus holding forth according to the urgency of the matter in hand. In no sense was this intended rudeness, for he was very well mannered – merely a very odd habit.

---

[13] Daymen earned about 12 shillings a week.

[14] Gerald Porter only discovered his full name after his death.

In later years, when he had lost all his teeth, Shepherd developed the odd, unconscious but irritating, habit of sucking his lips in very noisily. Gerald's memoirs tell how

> . . . our shepherd was a poor man with dogs, and they paid scant regard to his behests. 'Lie down, good dog', he would say, and accordingly the dog would rush about and bark more furiously than ever. (I once heard a Hampshire shepherd bawl out to his barking beast, 'Shut the gurt mouth jist' and he shut it forthwith.)

> My father told the tale that soon after Shepherd came they were handling sheep and the dog was very forward and took no notice whatever of his Master, so my father hit him, intending to land the stroke square on his back. However, Scot drew back and received the blow on his snout with such force that the stick was broken and a prolonged howl arose. Father told the Shepherd that he didn't intend this, but the latter replied, 'It won't hurt 'un' – nor did it, and he (the dog) was soon as bad as ever. The best dog he ever had was a little bitch, Bessy, who served him well for years. But he must have walked miles and miles to round up the flock as he could not trust – or control – his dogs.

When he arrived at Manor Farm John Winfield

> . . . found a flock of Cotswolds, the breed so common on the hills at that time. Large white-faced sheep with very heavy fleeces of coarse fibre and with flesh much interlarded with fat, so that, with a change in the public

taste both with food and clothing, it will be easily understood that such a class of sheep lost favour. But they remained valuable for crossing purposes and the Holwell flock was graded up and produced a hundred or so ram lambs annually which were sold in East Anglia. He was devoted to his flock and would see that they were fed and cared for, rain or shine. Extravagant in feeding maybe – 'the poor things must have a bit of cake' . . . The cake bills soared.

Shepherd John Winfield

In an effort to keep feed bills for the sheep under control, Thomas West Porter sometimes had the haystacks built some distance from the turnip field where the sheep were folded. His theory was that the time and effort involved in fetching hay would curb Shepherd's instinct to indulge his flock. Shepherd usually had a pony and cart to help with the hauling but when he was on his own the load of hay 'tied in a long hair cord . . . looked like a miniature rick walking on two spare legs'. The Holwell shepherd had three flocks to manage: the flock of breeding ewes and the fattening flock, which consisted of home-reared and bought-in 'tegs' (lambs between one and two years old, both ewes and castrated ram lambs, known as wethers). There was also a small flock of breeding rams, to which was added two or three bought-in rams yearly.

> In the autumn, at the beginning of the farming year, the 'tegs' were penned or folded on fields of early turnips. 'Tankard' turnips followed the early ones, this shape being preferred as they did not roll about in the autumn and winter mud when being eaten. About Christmas they would go on to swedes – these were cleaned and sliced with a cutter and fed into the troughs. All this involved much more labour and an under-shepherd was employed, usually a young fellow qualifying for a shepherd himself.

These fat lambs were sold off in the spring. After harvest the ewes were turned out to clear up 'seed leys[15], stubble, late grass and so on, and as these were finished they too would come on to roots'. They

---

[15] Cotswold 'seeds' were a mixture of clover and rye grass.

were penned closely on turnips, and given too many. On this diet, 'they got fat' and 'looked well' but the percentage of losses at lambing times both with the ewes and lambs was often 'alarmingly high'. When he began to farm on his own account, Gerald Porter went over to a regime of grass feeding with 'perhaps a few roots and about a month before lambing a small allowance of crushed oats and cotton cake'.

After Christmas the breeding flock was brought into the ewe pen. Lambing began early in the New Year and lasted almost until the end of February. The shepherd was on duty round the clock, snatching what rest he could in his cabin in the ewe pen. Graham recalled:

> The ewes were put in an open yard, sheltered with gate-topped hurdles thatched with straw. Round part of the yard ran a covered thatched shed called a bowsin in which the shepherd made small pens in which to put the newly born lambs with their mothers. After a day or two, if all went well, they were drafted into another open sheltered yard where they remained for about a fortnight or until the lambs were strong enough to be taken out into a field of swedes, having access to a sheltered pen littered with dry straw for them to take shelter in if the weather was cold and wet.
>
> The flock was provided with a strip of fresh swedes each day by moving the hurdles forward, there being a creep hurdle in the fence through which the lambs passed but not the ewes, so that they could have the best of the food. The earliest born and best of the ram lambs were fed as well as possible to be fit for sale for breeding purposes in the summer months. Sufficient ewe lambs to

replenish the flock were kept, the remainder of the lambs being fed on swedes which had been pitted in small heaps and cleaned and then cut into small pieces by a turnip cutter which had to be moved from heap to heap, not a very easy job for the under-shepherd, especially in wet muddy weather. I wonder what the young men of today would think of such a job?

Gerald takes up the story of the lambing year:

Then as the lambing was about over, it would be time (say in late February) to get the first draft of tegs ready for sale and, in those days, this was no small job . . . Thirty or forty would be brought in from the roots to be 'belted'. Having such long wool, they were laden with 'clegs', lumps of mud, especially round their rumps and under their bellies. Of course, the obvious way was to cut this off with shears, but such proceeding was strictly 'verboten'. So two men laid the 'teg' on its side and, if the lumps were wet and sticky, pulled them apart (a dirty job) and, if they were hard and dry, the men had woollen mallets and a flat piece of wood, and pounded the lump to pieces. It was a tedious job, but every bit of wool must be saved and labour was cheap.

Next the tegs were driven slowly to Signett[16] to be washed. I think the shepherd superintended this. It was a shock for the teg to be flung into cold (February) water

---

[16] Pronounced Sign-ett.

. . . Very rarely one's throat would have to be cut and hurried back to be 'dressed'. After washing they were kept on a dry ley and well fed and, in about a week's time, housed in a warm cart shed and shorn. This proceeding continued through the spring, and no sheep left the farm without 'leaving his wool behind him'.

The remains of [wash pools] may yet be found where a rivulet or stream [gives] life and interest to the locality. The purpose of such pools was, of course, for the washing of the sheep previous to their being shorn . . . unwashed wool was as rare in my youth as washed is today.

The pool was formed by building up the sides of the stream for the required distance . . . [It was] usually large enough to hold three or four sheep [and] about as wide as a young fellow could jump. The water flowed in over some sort of a hatch and there would be something similar at the outflow, and, in addition, a rail to prevent the sheep swimming out too soon . . . In some cases there were fixed collecting pens, otherwise hurdles had to be erected. It was no easy job to get old ewes into these pens, knowing as they did, what was before them . . . Two men would throw the sheep in and the shepherd and another man would rub them well with long handled 'crutches'. I believe, in some of the larger streams, the men would stand in [the water] with waders on and thus handle the sheep.

There was a slope, with perhaps rough steps, [at] one . . . corner of the pool and up this the washed animal walked (or rather staggered, for a Cotswold with its fleece soaked had a heavy weight to be carried and often had to be assisted). They had to go through twice. The second penning, with their fleeces wet to boot, was no mean effort . . . The old dog barked himself hoarse and an impetuous shepherd lad might get washed himself . . . After the second immersion there was not, as a rule, much dirt left in the fleeces. The Cotswold, with their white faces and legs, looked particularly clean after the ordeal. There was a constant flow of fresh water through the pool but, even so, the liquid got very thick and discoloured if the sheep were at all dirty, as they often were . . . It gave the few small trout that were usually to be found in such streams a very unpleasant time, and the farm stock too, if a watering place was not far downstream.

In our little Shill valley, the first pool was at Westwell. It is still to be seen with the spring of water from the Vicarage garden running into it. But the flow [today] is not much for the hundreds [of sheep] that must have been washed there years ago.

The next was at Signett, which we used from Holwell. This was a good pool with good collecting pens kept up by the Bradwell Grove Estate, but the water was often low, especially after water was taken out from the spring [which fed it] to supply the House and Estate. So we sometimes went to Shilton, where there was much more water – a really good pool which, however, was not kept in much repair and had no pens. It seemed to belong to no one in particular, though old John James

said in his complimentary way, "Twere auld Ike's concarn'
– that is, it might be owned by Mr Isaac Stratton, who
lived at the Manor Farm. As I afterwards lived there, I
always considered it my property and I think made a
small charge for its use, but this more for the hurdles . . .
provided [than for the use of the pool itself].

[A wash pool] is [still] to be seen in Lower Slaughter
in very pretty surroundings, the little stream with yellow
iris, and at Snowshill on the small rivulet that flows down
to Broadway is a very curious pool – circular, not very
large, I have never seen one quite like it. Of course there
must be scores of these pools in a famed sheep district
such as the Cotswolds once were, and they are worth
noting.

In March or April the young lamb's tails were docked: if they were
allowed to remain long they inevitably became caked in dung and
offered an ideal breeding ground for blow flies. On some Cotswold
farms it was the custom to 'tail' lambs on Easter Tuesday. The tails
were often skinned and cooked and were considered a real delicacy.

Weaning followed, when, for a time, there was a great
hull-a-ba-loo in the sheep world. The ewes then would be
washed and shorn, and any unfit for further breeding
drafted out.

At the beginning of summer, to safeguard his flock against the torments
of ticks and maggots, the shepherd brought the 'Dipper' in.

Each sheep has to be lifted into an oblong, deep tub and held there by the shepherd and another man for the requisite minute. The shepherd kept one hand over the sheep's mouth in case it swallowed any of the poisonous liquid . . . After a minute in the tub the sheep was passed on to a draining board with sparred sides, which sloped towards the tub so that the liquid ran back. At one time, I believed, the sheep . . . was laid on spars and the dip pressed by hand out of the fleece so that altogether it was a hard, dirty, hot job. This draining affair was fixed up in a long cart that the dipper brought. He travelled from farm to farm and mixed his own dip, a crude and uncertain concoction.

The Shepherd would not have much share in the haymaking, though following it with interest, for on the quality of the hay a good deal would depend for his precious charges. He would find plenty to do, being pretty much single-handed at this season, and, if the ram lambs were being reared, they wanted a lot of feeding and attention. They, as most of the lambs, would be on vetches[17], but for the rams these must be mown and fed into racks – a laborious job. As a matter of fact, these rams were often over-fed, especially by a man such as ours, and in the effort to get premature maturity, stamina suffered. It was so with pedigree stock generally at that time.

Then before sale, in early August, these rams had to

---

[17] Legumes.

be coloured yellow. This was done by penning them closely and pouring water mixed with ochre over them with a watering pot with a rose on. After such an operation the sheep themselves looked decidedly jaundiced, and the old dog too, if he got in the way. It was really rather absurd, this colouring – but there it was, and is. Cotswolds were never 'trimmed', only their tails were 'squared'.

Sometimes a load would be taken to Oxford or Cirencester Ram Fairs, but with no great success. The shepherd had to go with them, and I remember him returning once very dejected, and in reply to my enquiring how he had got on, saying bitterly 'never sold nur a one'. It was much better to sell the hundred or so at one price to a dealer who had them away in drafts for the East Anglian Fairs where a demand existed, and still does, for crossing purposes.

During harvest our man would be fully occupied with the flock and very rarely handled any sheaves.

Arthur Street described the strategy employed on his father's farm in *Farmer's Glory* thus:

. . . if the occasion were desperate, and another hand must be got somehow, the Shepherd was the last resort. You didn't send the foreman to see if the shepherd could get away for an hour or two. That would have been to court disaster. The sheep would have been in such a critical state that if the shepherd left for a moment, they would all be sure to die. Neither was I sent. Youth hadn't the tact required for such a ticklish operation. Oh no! That was a job for the Guvnor, and from the rick we would see Tommy[18] being urged to his most furious speed up the far slope towards the sheep fold. Having arrived, my father talked sheep, sheep and nothing but sheep, thus relegating the harvest to an unimportant detail unworthy of mention. After a bit the shepherd would be sure to say: 'And how be getten on wi' the carrying zur?'

'Pretty fair, shepherd. We're a bit short handed today. I'm on my way down to the village to see if I can pick up another man.'

'Well, zur, I be about straight yer just now, in a manner o' speaking. Ud it be any good if I were to gie a hand for an hour or two?'

And back to the harvest field would come Tommy, hauling both the Shepherd and my father, who had achieved his object without mentioning it.

Returning to Gerald's memoirs of Manor Farm –

. . . as the season advanced, the breeding flock required more attention. Two or three fresh rams were introduced each year – great animals, white-faced, long woolled and far too fat. They were generally purchased at the two Ram Sales still held on the farm where they were bred – Uncle

---

[18] The pony which pulled Mr Street's trap.

Lane's[19] at Broadfield and Mr Robert Garne's at Aldsworth.
Other breeders were sending their rams to the fairs, as a
home sale was an expensive affair and as the prices for
Cotswolds declined, could not very well be afforded.

Further as to these Sales. The only ones I went to
were at Aldsworth, to which my father took me as a boy.
It would be at the end of July and there would be a large
gathering of Cotswold farmers (not all necessarily
sheepmen) with one or two from Norfolk, where some
flocks of Cotswolds were kept. The spacious entrance
yard was filled with all sorts of horse-drawn vehicles and
Neal the groom had a busy – and lucrative time. A large
marquee was erected on the lawn and hospitality was
dispensed on a lavish scale – a courtly old butler (I forget
his name) from Filkins[20] being more or less in charge.
What I remember best was the delicious cream cheese. Of
course, plenty of 'drink' was going, but I cannot call to
mind any excess in this way, probably most of the guests
could stand a good drop. I need hardly say that the
shepherds, who often went with their masters to these
sales, were likewise lavishly entertained, in a large barn
usually. It was well to keep in with the shepherds.

The host was Robert Garne, a man in his prime, at
this time, a typical Cotswold farmer of the old style, sturdy
independent and somewhat haughty in manner, but [he]
would do any neighbour a good turn. He was a bachelor,

---

[19] Gerald's grandmother's brother.

[20] A nearby village.

his two sisters keeping house for him. They were Victorian ladies to a degree: Tory and C. of E. I remember them very well, for as a little boy I stayed with Aunt Susie[21], who had married William Garne, [their] nephew and lived near, so I was often taken to 'Uncle Robert's' house. They were always very kind to me, but I stood in considerable awe, as it was proper then that a small boy should . . . [Mr Garne] would go regularly to church in the morning but walk out as the sermon commenced.

Now as to the Sale. The rams – fifty to sixty – would be in groups of, say, half a dozen. The paddock was undulating, so the small pens were erected on the highest points in order that the sheep would show to the best advantage.

They were shearlings, that is about one and a half years old, and as they had been 'done' well all their lives, they grew to a great size and had very heavy fleeces, not having been shorn too bare in the early spring. They were always coloured the conventional yellow. Cotswolds had white faces and legs – the latter being bare of wool – indeed they were shaven in some cases, I have understood. A little splash of grey on the face was not objected to by some breeders indicating, they averred, a stronger constitution.

There was a large selling ring formed by hurdles, and, due justice having been done to the host's hospitality, the auctioneer – Arthur Acock – mounted the

---

[21] On Gerald's mother's side of the family.

rostrum. He commenced by thanking Mr Garne on behalf of everyone present, for his good cheer so lavishly dispensed (there was no formal speech making) and was sure he had never shown a better lot of rams. He then asked for bids, which he hoped would be generous etc. etc.

Number one ram was then brought into the ring and walked round – a good sheep but not the best – for like a good cricket captain, who does not put his best batsmen first, the sheepman keeps back what he considers his best rams till later, and often numbers five and seven were outstanding animals.

At the time of which I am writing Cotswolds were a little past their zenith when three figure prices were not unusual. I suppose twenty to thirty guineas would buy the best at the Sale we are speaking of, and the average would be in the teens – and soon afterwards not reaching this. And, eventually, Cotswold shearlings were almost unsaleable and lambs were sold instead, but not at these Sales, which had long ceased.[22]

Long credit was given, and I think some farmers did not pay for a year. It was an unhealthy custom. The Garnes were (rightly) sharper after their money, but easy-going men like Uncle Lane must have lost a small fortune in this way. Of course a man can give a good price if he doesn't intend to pay!

---

[22] Gerald's father's accounts show that he paid between 13 and 21 guineas for rams at these fairs during the 1870s and 1880s.

The rams were delivered any reasonable distance, so [for] the next few days a strong cob with a light cart . . . would be going round to the various farms in the immediate neighbourhood.

But we have wandered from our own Shepherd whom we had followed to the Harvest. Burford Fair is again coming round. Is he going to stay another year, and is the Master satisfied with his work? Well, as there appears to be mutual agreement, he stays, as we have already noted, till his working days are over.

Chapter Three
ARABLE FARMING

erald Porter's memory stretched back to the days of the oxen, which were used for ploughing in the Cotswolds after almost every other English region had gone over to horse power. He could just remember his father using oxen, although he was only about four or five years of age.

Four in single file usually made the team for a single plough – six in pairs for a double one, and I think for other cultivations they were worked double. They were great lumbering animals and seemed slower than they really were. One I can recall was named (for all bad names) 'Nimble'. Their harness, though much like that of horses, had important variations. Their collars slipped up the neck and were secured by a strap on the top, and the point of draught was higher in relation to the shoulder than with a horse. The mullens[23] had no bits and the blinkers were often very spreading. The harness never seemed to wear out for the sweat from the beasts kept it pliable, whereas that from the horse tends to dry up and crack the leather.

---

[23] A kind of bridle that incorporated blinkers.

At meal time the oxen would lie down in the furrow and chew the cud, unless indeed the byrefly came along, when they betook themselves to the nearest hedge with the utmost speed, plough and all . . . It was no joke disentangling half a dozen frightened oxen from plough and harness on a hot July day.

The cart-horse stable [was] a most important institution in those days of arable farming carried out by horses. It was a long building with room for twelve or fourteen horses; these stood in a long row with the manger and haycribs in front, and the much necessary harness hanging on pegs at the rear. The chaff and corn bins were at one end, the carter carrying the mixture in a sieve between each pair of horses. One never heard of him being kicked; they knew (the horses did) their man, and the reason of his frequent advances.

. . . The carter occupied a very responsible position on the farm, and rose early so that his team should be well 'baited'[24] fed and fitted for the day's work. He would be in the yard about 5.00 a.m. and let the horses in from their yards and boxes, feed and brush them down, in this being helped by one or two of his chief assistants, and then return to his breakfast and be again at the stable a little before 7 o'clock to receive orders from the 'Master', and pass such to his subordinates, for it was not stable etiquette to ignore the Carter, who in a large stable had numerous youths and boys under his control, and in this

---

[24] Fed.

way he acquired considerable experience in the management of men and affairs (my father always averred that a carter made a better farm foreman than a shepherd, as the latter is more or less a 'law unto himself' – there are exceptions of course).

The work arranged, harnessing followed. In those days 'single' teams were mostly worked and the horses had to be harnessed accordingly – 'forrust'[25], 'body'[26] and 'thiller'[27]. 'Body' was in the middle and the younger horses were usually placed there; the 'thiller' often being a wise old mare, who beyond pulling the plough out at the heads, continued to keep her 'togs' (chains) just taut enough to show that she was not slacking. The boys, of whom there were plenty, put the mullens on, usually having to climb into the manger to reach the horses' heads.

Three-horse team ploughing.

---

[25] The 'lead' horse.

[26] The powerhouse of the team.

[27] Or the 'tiller', used to steer.

But the working of horses in pairs soon began to come into vogue. This dispensed with the small boy drivers, who indeed, were kept at school longer, and it really was better for the horses as each had to do his (or her) share. In a single team one horse would pull a good deal of the load to which of course the lazier and more cunning ones had no objection. Then came 'double furrow' ploughs, and three horses abreast and one carter, a saving of two boys and one carter and three horses. Now (1943) a tractor draws 3 or 4 furrows and makes longer, perhaps double, hours of work.

It was interesting to see a dozen horses being assembled into four three-horse teams. They had a good drink at the stone water trough, and then were led to their appointed stations and thus left for the field, headed of course by the Carter's own team and followed by the others in strict order. It was unthought of, for instance, that the third carter should precede the second.

The boys led the 'forrusts' and all day long walked by the side of their team, their little legs must have ached badly ere 'shutting off' came, which would be about 3.30 in the winter and somewhat later at other seasons, indeed at haysel[28] and harvest, work proceeded till dark. In wet wintry weather the teams, on their return from work, would be ridden through the large shallow pond to clean their legs, which often in those days carried a lot of unnecessary hair. A cribful of hay was the first and safest

---

[28] When the hay was cut and saved.

Head Carter leads the teams for their day's work.

feed whilst the carters had their tea and then followed the evening baiting and much grooming as often the horses were very dirty and sweaty. The master often visited the stable at this time, when the work for the following day would be discussed, and 'turning out time' was about 7 pm – a fairly long day!

Then there were the days when the teams went 'on the road' delivering the much grain then grown; and for this there would be much burnishing of brasses etc. on the harness. Indeed the Carter often had sets of harness

75

specially for these occasions, and many ornaments were added. The 'martingales', a row of shining brasses attached to a broad band of leather that passed between the horses' fore legs, bells on the mullens, ribbons and so forth, all making a brave show of which the horses seemed as proud as their Carter and, be it confessed, oftentimes the master himself.

Railway facilities were becoming available about this time and stations within a few miles of most farms, but a fair proportion – especially of wheat – was hauled to the local mills, and in some cases a long journey was involved there.

The roads too were very indifferent, being made of the local limestone. They were soft and cut up badly in winter, hence hauling was a hard job and not infrequently the team would be a four-horse one: forrust, next-to-the-forrust, body and thiller. But to turn out three three-horse teams fit for the road taxed the resources of a twelve-horse stable as there were always some only fit for the land work: too old, too young, a bit lame and so forth.

On road journeys, the Carter carried a long smart whip (kept hung up in his cottage) with shining brass bands round the handle. It was seldom used on the horses. A 'bolton' of straw was carried on each load of corn to be bartered for 'a drop of summat' at the favourite pub. This was commuted, though, in some cases for a shilling a load, as the size of the bolton led to bickerings, never large enough etc., and I daresay sometimes the man who tied it and who may, as a boy, have been thrashed by the old carter, had his own back with the straw – in quantity I mean . . .

Even longer journeys were made in taking loads of Cotswold ram lambs to the fairs on the Berkshire and Wiltshire downs and from these both men and horses would return very tired.

The waggons were often painted a bright yellow with the farmer's name and address, and the date of the last painting inscribed boldly on the front. A man who cared for his implements would have one waggon painted each year. So that, with five or six of such vehicles, all were thus kept in a reasonable state of repair.

In his reminiscences Graham Lane Porter focused on the arable side of the work at Manor Farm, perhaps because he knew that his brother Gerald had penned an affectionate portrait of Shepherd Winfield and his work, perhaps because of his own preferences for working with machines. He left school at the age of fifteen, just after Christmas 1896, and started work on the farm

. . . under the tuition of my father. The farm of about 500 acres was mostly on stonebrash, with here and there some clay as the name of one field, Clay Furlong, would indicate. It was worked with about ten men and boys and a stable of 10 or 12 horses with very little machinery in my young days. The head carter had about three lads under him. The night before they would be going to the station to deliver corn or to take a load of sheep to market you would find them in the stable polishing the brasses with which to deck their teams. A pair of horses drew a single furrow plough in the early days and if a man could plough an acre a day it was considered a fair day's work.

We used to buy two Sussex colts each year and break them in at two to three years old and at the same time sell two at the age of four or five years, thus keeping a young team. The only thing against this was it was not always easy breaking in, and the young horses were more liable to be running away. To break them in they were harnessed with trace harness and put between two steady horses attached to a plough, and a man with a long plough rein attached to each side of the bit of the youngster would be ready to check him when he plunged. However, by the end of the day he usually began to settle down so that the service of one of the men could be dispensed with and eventually the carter and his plough boy managed by themselves.

My first remembrance of the way haymaking was done: the grass was cut with a scissor-type machine drawn by a pair of horses, and after lying in a swath for a day or two according to the weather, when it was getting somewhat dried on the top, all hands available were provided with a small hay rake to turn the swaths over and, if it was a stormy time, the tedious job had to be repeated until the grass was thoroughly dried and then put up in small heaps called cocks ready to be pitched on to wagons and taken to the rick and there pitched by hand on the rick. No elevator available, although after a time we invested in a Jarmin swath turner and a Roberts elevator. Both of these, although not so efficient as the present day ones, alleviated one of a lot of hard, sweating work.

Now to turn to a harvest scene. When the corn was ripe the first thing to be done was to make a clear way round the field so that the horses drawing the reaper did not tread the corn down. This was done by a man mowing a swath all round the field and tying the corn in sheaves. Usually this was done by piece-work, so much a chain length, then the side-delivery reaper drawn by two horses was able to start work. This machine had a metal

Corn cutting c. 1910.

platform attached to the cutter bar on which the severed corn fell and there were four revolving rakes which swept the corn against the knife and on to the platform taking the then severed corn off the platform and leaving it in small heaps. From these, two small handfuls were taken and [the stalks] twisted together to form a band in which two of the wads of corn were placed and tied to make a sheaf. This work was usually done piece-work at a price estimated to enable a man to earn rather more than his ordinary wage. A man who had a wife and children usually enlisted them to help him in some of this work.

The corn thus tied and stacked stood in the field to get thoroughly dry before being carted to a barn or rick. When ready for this the head carter and another man worked each side of the waggon pitching sheaves which were loaded by one of the stable boys usually, the horse being led from shock to shock by a small boy, and I remember when I was doing this having my toes stepped on more than once – not a very pleasant feeling. The load being completed, it was taken, often by a school boy on holiday, to the rick, here to be pitched sheaf by sheaf on the rick to a recipient who passed it to the builder, which was a skilled job, as if not correctly placed, there was a danger of the rick slipping out of place. After pitching heavy wheat sheaves all day long, especially overhead as the rick rose, one's arms ached. Our young men of today do not know much of this, do they?

The next thing was the thatching, which was done by a skilled man piece-work. It was a pleasant sight to see the countryside dotted with well-built thatched corn ricks, but these often got disfigured by rooks pulling off the thatch to get at the corn when they had difficulty getting their other food through snow and frost. Moreover, corn

ricks were a good shelter for rats and mice till thrashing
time when I have known literally hundreds of these trying
to escape the blows of sticks from many of the boys who
would gather round the rick on such an occasion, or the
jaws of the terrier waiting to tackle the big rats.

An entry in Graham's father's diary for July 1913 suggests that a
morning killing rats and mice was considered good entertainment for
visiting grandsons.

Now as to the thrashing of the corn. We had a portable
engine and thrashing drum which were moved by horses,
which, when the ground was wet and soft, was not an
easy job to get them to line up correctly for the long belt
connecting the engine and drum to stay on the pulleys
when in motion. Thus ready for action the sheaves from
the rick were pitched on to the drum to be taken by a
man who with a knife cut the bands and fed them into
the drum which beat the corn from the straw and, thus
severed, the corn passed over various sieves, eventually
falling into sacks. The chaff, having been blown by a
strong fan, was collected in big bags and taken to be put
in the dry to be fed to the stock. The straw fell on the
ground (before the elevator was available) and was
carried in big pitch forkfuls several yards to make a rick.
The corn was put in sacks, wheat in about two and a
quarter hundred weight sacks and barley two hundred
weight, and taken off and moved with a sack truck and
stacked nearby to be loaded into a wagon. This was done

by manual labour (no fork lift). Two men having a strong stick, balanced the sack on this, on lifting it from the ground, and hoisted it on the wagon, sometimes having the help of a push from a third man behind. A man on the waggon with a sack truck stacked the sacks close together. To complete this operation meant some hard work. The whole business of threshing was by no means a pleasant job, being very dusty, so that at the end of the day one was ready for a good wash or would have appreciated one of the present day's shower baths.

In my young days the only artificial fertilizer I can remember was superphosphate (no nitrogen), so to maintain the fertilization of the soil we were dependent on the dung cart, except for the so-called golden hoof[29]. The application of putting the dung on the land was a slow tedious job, two or three men with four grain forks loading it on to carts (no present day fork lifts) which, when full, were taken by a lad to the field where the carter, with a long handled drag, pulled the dung out in small heaps, evenly spaced, to be spread evenly over the field, this job often being done at a piece-work rate. It can well be understood that, by so little fertilizer being available, the yields were not very big. Moreover, there were no sprays for weed killing. The only method for this was hoeing between the rows of corn with a narrow four-inch hoe. From records of corn yields kept by my father during the 1880s, in 1881 the average yield for wheat per

[29] Allowing the sheep to spread their own muck.

acre was 4 quarters 2 bushels = 19 hundredweight 14 pounds, and for barley 4 quarters 7 bushels = 19 hundredweight 56 pounds – in other words, a little under one ton an acre[30]. Wheat for sale was weighed up at 63 pounds per bushel and sold by the quarter or 8 bushel, the price being between 30 and 40 shillings per quarter[31]. Barley weighed at 56 pounds per bushel and sold at about the same price or even less; somewhat different to the present day prices, but we must take account of the difference in rent in those days, some being as low as seven shillings and sixpence per acre[32]. Also the difference in the price of labour, wages being as low as ten or twelve shillings per week[33] with no half day holiday and only the fixed holidays during the year.

---

[30] Over 100 years later 3 to 4 tons per acre is not unusual.

[31] About £7 per ton (now about £120 per ton minus acreage payment).

[32] Now an average £60 per acre.

[33] Now an average £200 per week.

Chapter Four

HOW THE
LABOURER LIVED

erald Porter considered that for the carters, and perhaps for their passengers, too

. . . the most trying journeys were those involved in moving the households of labourers who changed their employ at Michaelmas and who, not infrequently, had to be fetched many miles to their new abodes. It was a common sight to see, perched on a load of household goods, the wife and a bevy of youngsters with usually a baby in arms. If it were a wet day, it was pathetic. And perhaps [there was] a dirty cottage awaiting them.

He recalled the arrival of Shepherd Winfield, his wife Eliza and their baby William at Holwell in 1872:

'Duke', young then but afterwards a very old favourite, was 'tiller' to the cart, and on the way home bolted, but nothing serious happened beyond much alarming Mrs Shepherd and the baby.

To illustrate the terms on which farmworkers were employed, Gerald quoted an entry from his father's farm accounts, 'hired Henry Watson as carter to have 12 shillings per week all the year round'. Gerald observed that sometimes wages were reduced during the winter. On top of his basic pay, Watson received '£1 extra for haymaking, £1 ditto for harvest and 1 shilling for every load of corn taken out'. Gerald assumed that 'a cottage rent free would be included, but such, being so well understood, would not be mentioned in the formal terms'.

The skills of carters, or ploughmen, as they were known elsewhere, were recognised. They were among the elite of the farmworking population and, as Gerald stressed, 'these farm wages were quite equal to those paid in my young days when 'day' men got 9 to 10 shillings per week and no cottage though the rents they paid for their cottages were . . . very small; 1 shilling or so per week . . . Old William Brunsdon said his father had 8 shillings per week. There were eight in a family needing eight loaves per week and this at one shilling per loaf. He has seen his mother cry because she had not enough food for her children.' The carters' privileges included year-round employment: 'Day' men were paid only when they worked. Illness or bad weather meant no pay.

It may well be asked how men lived and brought up their families – often large ones – on such small monetary pittances. That they did and usually creditably too, is a fact which perhaps merits a little further enquiry. First money went further than in more recent times, and there were not the ready opportunities and inducements to spend. Then there was a great deal of help in kind, call it charity if you will, but most farmers and their wives looked upon it as almost a sacred trust and obligation that their employees and poorer neighbours should be cared for as far as they were able to do so. For instance, as children, we were always encouraged to tell our parents of any need or sickness we might have heard of in the village. I have heard old women say to my mother, when she visited such a case, 'God bless that thur boy' because I had told mother about her.

In many cases a good deal of milk was supplied free by the farmer . . . though, at Holwell, where milk was scarce, it was only sent round during harvest time. This was a duty assigned to Evelyn[34] and myself as little tots, she with a small can for the smaller families and myself with a large one for the bigger families. How gratefully it was accepted and the cans rinsed out with hot water and returned to us. It involved several journeys for us, but of course short ones, the hamlet being so small.

Some charity was institutionalised. *Plum Money*, the intriguing phrase which Gerald took as the title for his memoirs, was a customary pre-Christmas bonus, found under one name or other in many parts of the country. The original plums, for which the money had been substituted, were the dried fruit which went into a Christmas pudding, fruit loaf or porridge. In some places, the farmers or the squire provided the flour too.

---

[34] Gerald's sister.

Manor Farm was the only farm in the tiny hamlet of Holwell, and on the morning of 21 December 1871, the first St Thomas's day that Gerald and Graham's father Thomas West Porter spent there, a deputation of 'village matrons' appeared at the back door to demand their rights as they had enjoyed them in the old days of Thomas's predecessor Mr Pinnell. The request came as a surprise – it had not been mentioned in the lease – and Thomas refused to pay out without further investigation. The old vicar (the living archive of the parish) confirmed the existence of the tradition but was able to reassure the new tenant that the charge fell on the owner of the land, not its occupier. The confusion had arisen because Mr Pinnell had continued to pay 'Plum Money' while he lived at Manor Farm even after he had sold the property to the Bradwell Grove Estate and stayed on as a tenant.

The flat day rate of pay did not tell the whole story:

A great deal of farm work at that time was by the 'piece' so that it was open for a man to earn more than 'day' pay, assisted, as he often would be, by an industrious wife, and, forsooth, these women must have had a hard life, looking after the house and the bevy of youngsters, a baby coming almost annually, and then field work. But many seemed to thrive on it, <u>vide</u> Mrs Tom Trinder who married at 18 and had sixteen children and was an excellent field worker and is still going strong at about 90[35].

Much of the corn would be hoed in the spring, for

---

[35] In his generation, Gerald was unusual in celebrating the work of the farm labourers' wives.

drills were coming into use. In many cases a man would own a drill and let it out, following it himself, the farmer finding the horses, of which four would be needed as the drills were heavy cumbersome affairs. The price for hoeing would be about five shillings per acre, [and] a man needed to put his back into the job to do much over half an acre per day – apart from what his wife would do. The hoeing not only cleaned the ground, but benefited the crop by stirring the soil round the roots. Root singling followed, often clashing with haymaking . . . It was a treat to see a good hand singling (cutting out as it was called) and, at this, often the women excelled and very few doubles or branches would be left to be dealt with in the 'seconding'. Of course, before machinery came in there would be the cutting both of hay and corn. The tying and stooking of the harvest was also a big 'piece' item.

Sometimes the hauling of the hay and corn would be let to the men at so much an acre. I never had any experience of the former, but did of the corn once or twice, and it worked well. One year when I had a good deal of land, I did so, and the harvest was got in about a fortnight. The weather was good and it was in the men's interest to push on, which they did. I can remember one morning going out soon after 5 a.m. and finding them hard at work on the wheat cart. They earned a lot of money during those two weeks, but the work was done, and the corn safely in, and we could get on with the autumn cultivation.

A skilled man could earn good money . . . at thatching, and often his wife would 'elm' for him and the way the [hay and corn] ricks were finished off in many rickyards was a credit to master and man. Hayricks were carefully tucked and corn ricks pared round the sides and often built on staddles[36].

About the last 'piece' job of the year was cleaning and pitting the roots in the field in smallish heaps to be ground for the sheep as they were penned over the land. But there was often not much more than 'day' pay [to be] made at this job, the days were short and the weather bad, and thus a good bit of time was wasted, which the workmen had to lose. I think the women (naturally) rather jibbed at this job, though old Betsey Parker used to say [that] when [she was] overtaken by a storm as she was root-cleaning, 'I just sets myself down under the old 'umbreller' and sings 'How sweet the name of Jesus sounds'.

Then each man had his garden and allotment, both well cultivated, and thus supplied his family with plenty of fresh vegetables and potatoes. A couple of pigs, too, usually inhabited what passed for a sty. One pig was supposed to pay for the meal bought to fatten the two, in fact the meal man expected the pig to pay his debt. The other pig of course 'came indoors', I mean after death, in the form of bacon and so on. They were generally a good

---

[36] The mushroom-shaped stones more often seen lining paths today.

weight, fifteen score or more[37] and so helped out the meat ration.

My father had a system of supplying the stockmen with a fat pig annually at a shilling per score below the market price. In this case they were not allowed to keep pigs as my father contended that the temptation would be present for them to use the food supplied for animals that passed through their hands. I daresay it was so in some cases, but I think all our stockmen were thoroughly honest and Christian men.

I remember once the old shepherd saying to me when I asked him when he was finished grinding his malt, just to see that the bin was locked, 'Don't trust me, Sir – don't trust me, trust the Lord'. He had mistaken my meaning, for he was the last man whose honesty one would have questioned. As a matter of fact, we were careful to keep the malt bin locked for usually half a dozen great cured hams were buried in the malt which gave such a flavour to them, and even in our little community there might be found those who did not distinguish between *meum* and *tuum*.

Three complementary accounts of the domestic economy of Oxfordshire labourers' families deserve to be read alongside Gerald Porter's.

Flora Thompson's 'memorial book' *Lark Rise to Candleford* is closest to *Plum Money* in its approach. *Lark Rise* 'tells of the life of an

---

[37] About 300 lb.

Oxfordshire hamlet in the 'eighties ' of the last century'. Lark Rise, or Juniper Hill to give it its real name, was at the opposite corner of the county to Holwell. It stood 'on a gentle rise in the flat, wheat-growing north-east corner of Oxfordshire', nineteen miles from the city. As Flora Thompson explained 'the ploughing, sowing and reaping were recent innovations. Old men could remember when the Rise covered with juniper bushes, stood in the midst of a furzy heath'. The Rise represented free enterprise on the part of early Victorian working men and their families who had squatted on the open heath. As the result of a court action in 1853, the cottagers had lost their claim to enjoy squatters' freehold and in the 1880's most Lark Rise families rented their cottages for a shilling or two a week.

The other investigations of labouring life in the county were formal surveys by social scientists. In 1975 Raphael Samuel published *Quarry Roughs: Life and Labour in Headington Quarry, 1860 – 1920. An essay in oral history*. Like *Lark Rise, Quarry* had its origins in a squatters' settlement on the 'waste' within easy reach of Oxford. Over sixty years earlier Benjamin Seebohm Rowntree, whose study of poverty in York at the turn of the century is a landmark in the history of social investigation in England, and his co-author May Kendall brought out *How the Labourer Lives*, the smaller scale rural counterpart of his work on York.

In Flora Thompson's 'poor people's houses', the homes of farm labourers, 'everybody had enough to eat'. 'The chief ingredients of the one hot meal a day' were the product of self help: 'bacon from the flitch, vegetables from the garden and flour for the roly poly'. The flour was made from the ears of corn left behind in the fields after the harvest and gleaned over a period of two or three weeks by the woman of the house and her children. These 'leazings', as they were called in Lark Rise, were 'thrashed at home and sent to the miller, who paid himself for grinding by taking toll of the flour'. But 'bread had to be bought, and that was a heavy item'.

Many Quarry men were employed in the building trade, others made a living with a horse and cart. Poaching played an important part in the community's economy. 'They was good rabbits, they was come off the clay ground, they was fat, beautiful rabbits', one witness told Samuel. In the autumn mushrooms and blackberries were gathered for sale. Pigs were fattened. A notable group of Quarry women took in 'gentry and college washing' on an industrial scale. For widows in Quarry, 'laundry work provided an independent alternative to going into the workhouse or dependence on parish relief'.

For Flora Thompson and for Raphael Samuel's witnesses from Quarry, the pig was the sacrificial hero of the labouring household. The smell from the Lark Rise pigsty was

> . . . a healthy smell . . . for a good pig . . . promised a good winter . . . The family pig was everybody's pride and everybody's business. Mother spent hours boiling up the 'little taturs' to mash and mix with the pot-liquor, in which food had been cooked to feed the pig for its evening meal and help out the more expensive barley meal. The children, on their way home from school, would fill their arms with sow thistle, dandelion and choice long grass or roam along the hedgerows in wet evenings collecting snails in a pail for the pig's supper. These piggy crunched up with great relish. 'Feyther', over and above farming out the sty, bedding down, doctoring, and so on, would even go without his nightly half-pint, when, towards the end, the barley-meal bill mounted until

'it fair frightened anybody'.

Sometimes, when the weekly income would not run to a sufficient quantity of fattening food, an arrangement would be made with the baker or the miller that he should give credit now, and, when the pig was killed, receive a portion of the meat in payment. More often than not one-half the pig meat would be mortgaged in this way, and it would be no uncommon thing to hear a woman say, 'Us be going to kill half a pig, please God, come Friday', leaving the uninitiated to conclude that the other half would still run about in the sty.

. . . When the pig was fattened – and the fatter the better – the date of execution had to be decided upon. It had to take place some time during the first two quarters of the moon; for, if the pig was killed when the moon was waning, the bacon would shrink in cooking . . . The next thing was to engage the travelling pork butcher, or pig sticker, and, as he was a thatcher by day, he always had to kill after dark, the scene being lighted with lanterns and the fire of burning straw, which at a later stage of proceedings was to singe the bristles of the victim . . .

After the carcass had been singed, the pig-sticker would pull off the detachable, gristly, outer coverings of the toes, known locally as 'the shoes', and fling them among the children, who scrambled for, then sucked and gnawed them, straight from the filth of the sty and blackened by fire as they were . . .

Then the housewife 'got down to it', as she said. Hams and sides of bacon were salted, to be taken out of the brine later and hung on a wall near the fireplace to dry. Lard was dried out, hogs' puddings were made . . . 'Them's better'n any o'yer oil-paintin's', a man would say, pointing at the flitches on his wall . . .

Raphael Samuel gives the following account of pig keeping at Quarry:

. . . [it] was the joint responsibility of the husband and the wife – one great source of feed being the allotments . . . while the other was cottage waste: (The pig served as both a dustbin and a sewer: one argument advanced in defence of cottage pig-keeping, when the question was debated before the Headington Parish Council in 1896, was that if the Sanitary authority did away with pigs they would be creating another nuisance in their stead, 'because the district was not like a town where all the rubbish was fetched away in the cart'.) Children too played a part, 'hunting for pig-nuts (acorns) . . . and foraging . . . for waste.

When the pig was killed, the woman of the house was involved in a whole series of manufacturing activities. 'Flere', the pig's jacket, was melted for lard . . . blood, gathered at the killing, was made into black puddings . . . chitterlings (the pig's innards) went in faggots . . . trotters into jelly for soup. The pig's head was preserved as brawn . . . ham and bacon were taken off the body and treated with saltpetre . . . When the salting was finished the pig was hung up on a wooden rack 'right across the room', for pieces to be cut off as they were needed. 'That were a better picture than an oil painting because . . . you could take it down and have your piece of it' . . . Once there, the bacon was freely available for the early morning breakfast, the luncheon basin . . . or the evening hot-pot. One popular dish made out of it was bacon 'clanger' (a roly-poly of bacon chopped up with sage and onion, and rolled in a suet crust). Another was 'shackles', the Quarry stew . . . home-cured bacon . . . and . . . cabbage.

Writing much closer in time to their observations, Rowntree and Kendall painted a much bleaker picture of life in poor men's houses, up and down the country. Things were worse in the south, where wages were lower; wages in Oxfordshire were the lowest in England. Couples with young children were in the saddest plight; standards of living improved as the man's wages were supplemented by the earnings of his wife and growing children. The two examples which follow come from Oxfordshire, though whereabouts in the county it is impossible to say since the investigators changed their witnesses' names and concealed their location to protect their identity.

Mr and Mrs Dewhirst had two sons, aged three and six months, and three daughters, aged six, four and a half, and two.

Mrs Dewhirst is still a young woman, though there are five children, the youngest only an infant. For years she has never been anything but tired; but she has a pleasant face and must have been an attractive girl. No doubt Dewhirst married her on 12s a week, hoping he would soon get a cowman's or horseman's place, or vaguely intending to leave the village. But the years pass and now to leave would be impossible . . .

Dewhirst is a steady capable fellow, who never touches beer, except when he has a glass given. Occasionally he earns a newspaper, or even another ounce of tobacco, by acting as barber. In his spare time he works on the allotment, for which he pays at the rate of 1d a week. The rent runs to 1s 7½d a week. The four-roomed cottage is clean and comfortable, though perhaps 'four-roomed' is too dignified a term. The second downstairs room is a kind of pantry-scullery, the second bedroom a landing into which the stairs open. But there is no lack of fresh air.

Mrs Dewhirst's food bill is illuminating. Threehalfpence a week for milk would seem extravagant, if one did not remember the baby. The cheap meat – 6d a pound – is, except on Sundays, when the wife and children have a taste, kept religiously for the breadwinner. 'Bacon and cheese are quite out the question.'

'You can't call it living; it's a dragging of yourself along', says Mrs Dewhirst with a certain amount of quiet bitterness . . .

Clean as the house is, the look of poverty is unmistakable. Nothing new has been purchased since the Dewhirsts became man and wife.

'I've never bought anything new since I married; but my sisters gave me some black when my father died, and they paid my fare to the funeral.'

Couples like the Dewhirsts confided to the investigators 'We don't live, we linger'.

Mr and Mrs Curwen had eight children: three sons aged fifteen, thirteen and four, and five daughters aged fourteen, twelve, ten, six and six.

The Curwens occupy two adjoining cottages, for one of which they pay rent weekly; the other is free. By this arrangement they have four bedrooms, two living rooms, and two attics, and, as there are ten of them at home, they are all pressed into service one way or another.

They may be regarded as a typical example of how a thrifty, hard-working family can live when several members of the household are earning. The wages are low. Mr Curwen only gets 15s weekly . . . But the eldest boy brings in 4s and the second son 3s weekly, while Mrs Curwen earns 3s 6d regularly for looking after her husband's three brothers, none of whom have faced the responsibility of marriage on a weekly wage of about 14s.

Curwen works hard for his 15s – from 5 a.m. to 7 p.m. with half an hour for breakfast and about three-quarters of an hour for dinner. He also goes twice on a Sunday to look after the horses . . .

The eldest girl will soon go out into service; but at present she is helping her mother with the care of the younger children . . .

There is no tobacco and no beer, unless Curwen should be treated. Shoes in this household are a very heavy item – not less than £2 yearly – even when

Mrs Curwen mends the children's shoes with her husband's old uppers. As for clothing – in the past few months new suits for father and the second son alone have cost 32s. But Mrs Curwen's own clothing consists of the cast-offs of some relative. If pence are ever given to the children, they are not spent on sweets but stored in the penny bank towards new clothing in the summer. It is a Spartan way of living even now; but before the boys began to earn, it must have been one long and uncompromising Lent.

Another source throws a little further light on how the Holwell labourer lived – the census returns of 1881 and 1891. The census data tend to support some of the conclusions reached by Rowntree and Kendall. The Brunsdons' situation in 1891 demonstrates a dilemma faced by the household in which the presence of a young child made it difficult for his mother to work alongside her husband on the farm. Given the choice between income and living space, Stephen and Eliza opted for income: they, their children, Louisa (twelve), Charles (ten), Elsie (six) and Frank (one) were sharing three crowded rooms with a boarder, Arthur Brunsdon.

Holwell also had its counterpart of the bachelor household of the Curwen brothers. In 1881 Philip Matthews, the son of Vincent, the old Manor Farm shepherd, and Mary, his wife, headed a household containing six unmarried children; their daughter May was away. Ten years later May was keeping house for her four bachelor brothers: Caleb, a thirty-nine-year old agricultural labourer; Selim (thirty-seven), a gardener; Ezekiel (thirty-five), a farm labourer; and Homer (twenty-six), also a gardener.

98

The three older brothers had been among the first hands hired by Thomas West Porter when he took on Manor Farm. Caleb came as second carter from Michaelmas 1871, the following year he was 'day man on man's wages'; 'Zekiel – as he appears in Thomas West Porter's notes – was 'ploughboy' in 1871, 'ox boy' in 1872 and simply 'Zekiel Matthews' in 1873. Selim, following in his grandfather's footsteps, was hired as undershepherd four Michaelmases running starting in 1871. Gerald observed that

> In spite of their poor material rewards, these men . . . took a lively interest in the farm – it was as much 'ourn' as the master's, with the stockmen it was 'my' sheep, 'my 'osses', 'my' cows and so forth. There was real respect – I had almost said affection – between the farmer and his men and in many cases very little change of employer or employee.

Clearly experience varied from district to district and employer to employer and the small number of Oxfordshire households which Rowntree and Kendall described may well have been no more representative of the county's labourers than the independent-minded Quarry 'roughs' or the families at Holwell who benefited from Gerald's vigilance and his mother's charity.

Part Two

THE LAST
GENERATION

Chapter Five

FARMING IN THE GREAT WAR

etween the First World War and the Second, the Porter family's centuries' long history as Cotswold farmers came to an end. The opportunity to purchase a good farm in north-east Hampshire, an option strongly favoured by his father-in-law William Butler, encouraged forty-year-old Graham Porter to take the major decision to leave Manor Farm at Holwell, which he had taken over from his father in 1910, and transplant his young family to Crondall in Hampshire, where his wife's family, the Butlers, farmed. Graham's departure from Holwell coincided with the prospect of a change of landlord when the Bradwell Grove Estate came on to the market in 1921 following William Henry Fox's death in December 1920. Graham's elder brother Gerald was the last of the Porter 'yeomen of the Cotswolds'. He remained at Manor Farm, Shilton, on the Oxfordshire/ Gloucestershire border until he sold up and retired from farming in 1939.

Selling up at Holwell, 1921.

In a poem dated August 1947, thirteen months before his death, Gerald contrasted the modern mechanical harvest with that described two centuries earlier, when the whole family went into the field together, even the baby at the breast:

> All day they ply their task with mutual chat,
> Beguiling each the sultry tedious hours.
> Around them falls in rows the sever'd corn
> And shocks arise in regular array.
> But when high noon invites a short repast,
> Beneath the shade of sheltering thorn they sit
> Divide the simple meal and drain the cask.
> The swinging cradle lulls the whimpering babe . . .
>
> *Anon*

By 1947 the harvest had become a solitary task performed by 'a man arrayed in a grimy overall' – the engineer responsible for the red Massey-Harris combine harvester.

> He moves the shroud and thus reveals
> Confused collection, chains and wheels,
> Levers and axles, all in gorgeous red array
> Yet so combined that several parts
> Together set by human art
> Make a complete machine.
> 'Tis heavy work, yet not good ale, but petrol first
> Quenches the monster's thirst . . .
>
> *Gerald Porter*

It would be natural to interpret Gerald's poem as evidence that the Porter family clung to the old ways of farming. This was not so. It was not Gerald, the eldest son of this generation, but his younger brother Graham who took over when their father gave up the tenancy after very nearly fifty years. This was a common pattern replicated in the Porter family, and in the wider community of tenant farmers, over the centuries. In an age and craft in which individual health, energy and enthusiasm rather than *anno domini* determined the age of retirement, farmers were often succeeded by a younger son.

The size of the farm Graham Lane Porter took on in 1910 – 450 acres – put him in the league of the bigger tenant farmers, men whose primary role was normally strategic, who employed foremen to support them. Graham, however, did not see the necessity for a foreman on this size farm, but his father-in-law, William Northcroft Butler, who farmed several thousand acres in north-east Hampshire, did do so.

Whatever the regime, the work for the day was usually arranged the evening before, but changes in the weather sometimes disrupted plans. Graham's children enjoyed the tale told about their Butler grandfather: one day when one of his men came to the door early in the morning to ask for some advice William Butler looked out of an upstairs window and said he was just having a wash but would be down in a minute. The surprised response was 'Beant dirty be ye?'

As the first entry in his foolscap account book testifies, Graham 'commenced farming at Manor Farm, Holwell, on September 29th 1910, with live and deadstock valued as under

	£	s	d
15 horses and colts	311	0	0
53 cattle	524	10	0
421 sheep	819	9	0
(a mixture of Cotswold and Downs)			
34 pigs	64	15	0
Agricultural Implements	320	18	0

To set himself up in business, Graham 'borrowed off T. W. Porter' – his father and predecessor in the tenancy – '£400 at 5% interest per annum which is invested in the stock'. (This he paid off, in two instalments, in December 1914 and April 1917.) 'Cash in hand and invested' amounted to £534 16s 4d. The handover from father to son was evidently thoroughly business-like. In the autumn and winter of 1910-11, Graham purchased barley and oats, winter vetches, peas and beans, grass seeds and cake (animal food) from 'T.W.P.' 'Sundries bought' from 'T.W.P.' in the first autumn included miscellaneous ironmongery, nails, wire and binder twine; poultry: 37 old hens and 2 old cocks, 3 pullets and 44 pigeons; 4000 cabbage plants. On 14 November Graham settled J. Wells's bill for painting his name on the farm waggon. The transition from one generation to the next was complete.

Of course, a farm is more than the inventory of its live and deadstock – the quality of the land is significant. A parish-by-parish survey of the soils of Oxfordshire, undertaken by C. G. T. Morison, Lecturer in Agricultural Chemistry at the University of Oxford, and published in 1914, gives a positive report of Holwell. The Holwell soil was stonebrash – 'excellent sheep and barley land'.

> It is essentially a sticky soil which resents cultivation when wet and is difficult to deal with if tilth has once been lost. In spite of this, it is most useful sheep land. Sheep grow bigger and fatten better upon this land than any other soil in the country.

As an old Oxfordshire farmer told Morison's collaborator, John Orr, 'The best land is where the best farmer is' and the farmer's strength, in the Oxfordshire definition at least, depended on the quality of his land, his own skills and access to adequate capital. Setting up in business was a test of satisfactory reserves. When Graham summarised his 'receipts and expenses for the three quarters of a year ending June 30th 1911', expenses outran receipts by £500, all but a few shillings. The outgoings included all the household expenses (tradesmen's bills amounted to £101). In spite of the loss he had to pay over £13 in Income Tax, a similar sum in Land Tax, a Poor Rate of £38 and 4s 2d House Duty. This was the year in which he bought the Massey-Harris binder referred to earlier; it cost £29 from Leigh & Sons.

Graham's half-yearly rent bill amounted to £328 18s 6d. The number of men he took on is not given. The annual summaries of outgoings give an overall figure for expenditure 'by wages': in the first nine months of his tenancy at Manor Farm he paid out £287 11s 5d. The average farmworker's weekly wage in Oxfordshire on the eve of the Great War was 14s 11d but the arithmetic is complicated. Higher wages were paid to specialists, the shepherd and the carter for instance. The incalculable cost of piecework and the bad weather, when men hired by the day could not work and were not paid, need to be taken into account.

By June 1912 there was 'a balance in hand of £222 4s 8 ½d'. Inevitably, farm profits fluctuated. In 1912-13 profits were down to £136 and in 1913-14 they were up to £473 10s 4d. The influence of the Great War is seen in increased profits in the next five years: in 1914-15 Graham made an estimated profit of £993; and in the following year, £1345. In 1916-17 profits were at their highest at £1857; but were down slightly in 1917-18 at £1536. The next year, 1918-19, they rose to £1657.

In 1920 his profits slumped to £583, although sales of wheat, barley and sheep were still good. An adverse balance of wages to income is a partial explanation. But the run of earlier figures suggests that Manor Farm had not only good soil but a farmer well able to extract a satisfactory return from it, once he had got himself established.

It has to be acknowledged that Graham benefited from the increasingly favourable economic climate. The deep depression which hit English farming in the late 1870s was over by 1910. The pattern of farming which was practised at Manor Farm between 1910 and 1920 was a traditional Cotswold regime, fundamentally the same as that which Graham Lane Porter's predecessor at Holwell had applied when Arthur Young, Secretary to the Board of Agriculture, reported on farming in Oxfordshire in 1813, almost sixty years before Graham's father, Thomas West Porter, crossed the county boundary from Gloucestershire.

In spite of the prominence of sheep, Manor Farm had very few permanent pastures. The sheep played the part they had played in the economy of many a mixed farm back as far as the middle ages – a source of profit from their flesh and fleece as well as a means of enriching the soil with their dung. These ewes and lambs were not therefore permitted to roam open walks: they were penned up and moved on as they exhausted the turnips or swedes or the ryegrass and clover on which they were folded. Their diet was supplemented with what Graham lumped together as 'Artificials': lamb food, linseed and cotton cakes.

The feed crops for the sheep were grown in rotation with grain crops (wheat, oats and barley) as they had been since the eighteenth century. The practice at Manor Farm fitted into the pattern of land use observed in the Cotswolds by A. D. Hall and his companions, three men in an automobile – more precisely, three agricultural experts in a Leon Bollee, who toured England in three successive summers before the Great War to bring the readers of *The Times* up to date on the state of British farming. It was in 1911, the year of George V's coronation, just as Graham approached the first anniversary of his tenancy of Manor Farm, that what Hall called their *Pilgrimage of British Farming* reached the Cotswolds. (The commentary is taken from the book based on his collected articles.) 1911 was a bone dry year.

To match the drought of 1911 taxed the memory of the oldest farmers, 1895, 1887, 1874, 1863 being variously referred to, according to the age of the speaker. Over much of the country no rain to count fell between Easter and the Coronation[38] and that slight break in the weather was soon succeeded by the even fiercer heats of July . . .

As we left London on the 21st of July harvest was in full swing in the Thames valley . . . in one place wheat was being threshed in the field . . . In 1911 the corn stood like a regiment: the wheat a shining red gold and the barley almost dead white.

Much of the country was parched. The Wiltshire downs . . . were very white and blinding in the sun-glare and the drought . . . The early spring had been too dry and the crops had never got a hold . . . On the heights the sun had scorched the grass to the roots.

In the Cotswolds by contrast,

. . . the effect of the summer's drought was less apparent than in any county we had seen . . . Most of the country was under the plough but the clover was green and luxuriant, and the root crops were all that could be wished, growing vigorously with scarcely a miss perceptible. Late-sown oats were still quite green and looked like making yields of over average, so heavy and well filled were the heads, even if the straw was short.

---

[38] 22 June 1911.

As Hall informed his readers,

> The Cotswold farmers follow a very normal four-course rotation. Two corn crops are sometimes taken after ley[39], which itself is often left down for two years on the heavier soils; occasional fields of vetches and lucerne vary the cropping but we saw neither peas nor beans. Paring and burning the stubble is also a practice not often met with in other districts.
>
> Horned stock is not abundant and we were much surprised to traverse the whole ridge without seeing a single Cotswold sheep, though there were Hampshire and Oxford Downs in plenty. Yet the Cotswold sheep once possessed a position in the export market, being valuable for crossing when both wool and mutton were wanted together. Big, white-faced, long-woolled, a little coarse perhaps, the Cotswold is perhaps the most typical modern representative of the long-woolled race which has been differentiated into so many local breeds; and its value both for home and for export lies not only in its long wool but in the hardiness which has come from many generations on the bleak uplands. But, like many of the other big breeds, it is now suffering a little from the increasing demand for small and fine joints in the modern diminishing household, moreover, it has a reputation for coarseness in the wool . . .

---

[39] Arable land temporarily sown with grass seeds or a mixture of grass and clover or lucerne. It provides better grazing than permanent pasture, which is usually confined to parkland or areas which are difficult to cultivate.

Graham Lane Porter, as we know, remained loyal to the local breed – the second of his given names commemorated the Porter family's connection with another line of Cotswold yeomen celebrated as champions of the Cotswold breed.

Leaving the sheep aside, Graham was a far from conservative farmer. When he took on the tenancy in 1910, Manor Farm was worked by horses. And, if the sheep are the stock which dominate the farm accounts, it is the horses which come across as individuals. Prince, the cart horse, was the first to be sold off the farm; he went in September 1912 for a mere £6, almost certainly at the end of his working life. Good farm horses, especially mares with breeding potential were worth much more. Two mares bought in 1915, Flower and Smiler, cost Graham £112 4s. In 1916 he took the bold and forward-looking decision to buy a motor tractor.

The outbreak of the Great War in 1914 had meant competition for working men and horses. The fields had long been losing young men with no family ties to the towns where they took up work which rewarded their skills with horses and hand tools more highly than farm work. Some of them went further afield to the newer and more open societies of North America, Australia, New Zealand and South Africa. When the war came, the young, fit and adventurous selected themselves for the trenches. From 1916 men aged between nineteen and thirty were liable for conscription. The army's demand for horse power, added to those of carriers, draymen and horse-omnibus companies, helped to push up the price of horses.

The vagaries of the weather added to the farmers' anxieties by reminding them that they were at the mercy of the unpredictable English climate. The task of bringing in the first harvest of the War in 1914 was eased by a prolonged spell of fine weather but the following year rain delayed the autumn cultivation. Bad weather hampered the spring work in 1916 too. Later in the war, recognising the vital importance of winning the campaign for the harvest, the army was prepared to release soldiers, but at what farmers must have regarded as prohibitive rates of pay: four shillings a day for a six-day week, as against the regular Oxfordshire wage of 15 shillings a week.

The motor tractor was not the universally-approved answer to this accumulation of problems. Witnesses heard by a Committee appointed by the Board of Agriculture to investigate the future of farming were strongly divided on the virtues of mechanisation. Tractors were regarded as unreliable; spares were hard to get hold of; men with appropriate engineering skills were in short supply – and, with the war, the competing demands of the army and the munitions factories had exacerbated the situation. Even when they were in good working order, tractors presented problems: gates and barn doors had been designed for horse-drawn implements, tractors required a bigger turning space. No heavy pneumatic tyres were available, tractors churned up the road surfaces.

But, perhaps most significant of all, going over to tractor power required a revolution in thinking. Horses reproduced themselves; much horse feed was home grown. Not only did a tractor represent a big initial outlay, everything it needed had to be bought in. Many farmers seem to have preferred to carry on as best they could with a diminished work force. The first English tractor, the Ivel Agricultural Motor, designed by Dan Albone, went into production in 1902. It met with critical acclaim then – and since. The *Journal of the Royal Society of Agriculture* published an enthusiastic report in 1903; the Judges of the Royal Show awarded the Ivel a Silver Medal in 1904. Modern enthusiasts have described it as 'more a motor car than a traction engine', even the 'Benz' of tractors, in tribute to the originality and elegance of Albone's solution to the technical challenge of tractor design. The company went out of business shortly after the Great War. The market for agricultural machinery was depressed as farmers' incomes fell; converts to mechanised farming had relatively new tractors and the die-hards who had been reluctant to embrace change during the war years were unlikely to lay out capital in the economically harder time of peace. Even as late as 1930 there was a resistance to tractors.

Graham Lane Porter, unlike many of his farming contemporaries, had experience of the internal combustion engine. For solo use, he had traded up from a bicycle to a motorbike and, in March 1916, he had purchased a 1915 15-20 h.p. Studebaker from his father-in-law. Six months later, on 1 September 1916, he invested in a tractor – not the elegant English Ivel but a 16 h.p. Mogul, manufactured by International Harvester. The Mogul was an 'American Primitive', a clumsy-looking snub-nosed machine but, in the opinion of experts on early tractors, 'outstandingly reliable and long-lived'. The tractor, together with a three-furrow plough from Ransomes of Ipswich, cost £315. A waterproof cover added £1 7s 6d to the bill. Graham also bought a 17-tine Massey-Harris cultivator for £16 12s and a set of chain harrows for four guineas. He invested in a 400-gallon oil tank – the tractors ran on fuel which, at a shilling a gallon, was less than half the price of the petrol used in his car. Expenses on the tractor account for the first year of mechanised work at Manor Farm added up to £432 13s 7d, including a modest £5 spent on repairs. His experience of the Mogul evidently confirmed his enthusiasm for mechanical farming. In 1920 Graham bought another tractor, a secondhand Titan, for £210. The next year he bought a secondhand Austin tractor for £363 2s 6d.

The layout of Graham's cashbook graphically brings home the economic novelty of tractor work. Entries for 'Horses' sit on opposite pages, 'Horses Bought' on the left, 'Horses Sold' on the right. The entries for 'Tractor Account expenses' occupy a left-hand page facing another list of undiluted costs, 'Motor Account Expenses'. With the arrival of the tractor, Graham dispensed with three horses: Lion and Dragon went for £79 apiece; Captain for £31. Graham's note of commission charged on these prices suggests that they were sold at auction.

In November 1916 Graham and his elder brother Gerald jointly invested in a Bomford and Evershed Thrashing Drum (thrashing was the real test of a tractor's power) at a cost of £105, plus a further £5 10s for a drum belt. The brothers hired the drum from each other for 10s a day. The 'Thrashing Machine Account' thus took a reassuringly traditional form: money paid out was balanced by money coming in. In the year which ended on 30th June 1917, Graham paid out £11 for 22 days' use of the drum and received £15 10s for '31 days thrashing at Shilton'.

Chapter Six

FAMILY LIFE

*I*n 1900 Gerald, the eldest of Thomas West Porter's seven children, was twenty-seven and farming on his own account at Shilton Downs, two or three miles from Manor Farm, Holwell, where he had been born and bred and where his father was still tenant; he walked there and back, morning and night. He soon moved to The Lawn at Shilton where he began married life in 1902. His bride was Marian Emily Bodman, the daughter of Benjamin Bodman, a farmer from Calne in Wiltshire. Like the Porters, they were members of the Exclusive Brethren, who sought to lead a life of New Testament simplicity. The Brethren were inspired by a brilliant Irishman, John Nelson Darby, born in 1800. Darby was ordained priest in the Anglican church but resigned in 1827, having come to the conclusion that institutional churches had no scriptural foundations. Exclusive Brethren avoided contact with the secular world. Their determination to shun members who deviated in doctrine or practice has led to periodic splits in the movement and bitter divisions within families.

Gerald and Marian Porter had three children: Thomas Leslie Bodman, born in 1902; Gerald Arthur, born in 1907 (both boys were known by their second names); and Hilda, who was born in 1911. Towards the end of May 1913 Marian was staying with her parents when she became ill. An infected tooth had led to septicaemia – blood-poisoning – and her health deteriorated rapidly. Today the infection would be treated with antibiotics, but in 1913 it proved fatal: she died within a matter of days, on the 3 June, aged thirty-four.

Shilton.

Gerald Porter and his little family moved to Manor Farm, Shilton, in 1914. Like his father before him, Gerald remarried after his first wife's death. On 28 October 1917, less than three weeks after their father's death, Gerald's sister Lizzie wrote in her little pocket diary: 'Gerald told me of his engagement to M.H.'. Gerald married Miss Mary Hoare, his contemporary, the following year.

Marian and Gerald on their engagement, 1900 – Marian was to die only 13 years later, the result of septicaemia.

THE PORTER FAMILY, SEPTEMBER 1911. Standing left to right: Douglas Hindley, Harold Hindley, Graham Porter, Lizzie Porter. Seated left to right: Evelyn Hindley with baby Edith, and Eustace (Tom) and Amy Hindley in front; Edith (Edie) Porter, Edith Porter with baby Frank, Thomas West Porter with Dora Hindley on his knee, Kathleen Hindley, Ann Porter, Gerald and Marion Porter with Leslie (left), Arthur and baby Hilda. (Harold and Evelyn Hindley had just one more child, Esther, born in 1914; Graham and Edith had eight more children.)

Gerald's younger brother, Graham Lane Porter, met his wife-to-be on the platform at Alvescot station in June 1908, not long after her nineteenth birthday. Edith was the daughter of William Northcroft Butler and Sarah Jane who, since the early 1890s, had been members of the Exclusive Brethren – they had come into contact with Brethren through Dr Ryland, who had looked after Sarah Jane when she was seriously ill following the birth of her first child, Percy William, in 1887.

Percy, Edith and their sister Ruth were all born at Deane near Basingstoke. In 1891 the Butler family moved to Penn Croft, at Crondall in Hampshire, a farmhouse built in 1881. The household at Penn Croft grew rapidly: Herbert Northcroft was born in 1891, Mary in 1893, Frank a year later, Maria May in 1897, Lucy the following year, Philip George in 1900 and Muriel Jane in 1905. By the end of the nineteenth century a family of ten would have been considered unusually large. The tendency for couples to limit the number of children they brought into the world had been pioneered by households headed by gentlemen of private means and professionals – officers in the army and navy, medical men and lawyers – but by the 1890s it had taken hold at almost every social level. It would be natural to assume that Brethren regarded the birth of children as providential, confident that God would provide. But the pattern of big families was not universal among them. Patricia Beer, the daughter of a railway clerk, and brought up in an Open Brethren[40] family in Exmouth between the wars, recalled that in the Brethren community there 'many couples had one child, few had more than one, and there was a considerable proportion with none at all'. Indeed one couple openly acknowledged that they had deferred their marriage until the prospect of children was past.

---

[40] Less strict branch of Plymouth Brethren.

The Butler family outside Penn Croft, Crondall, around 1908. Left to right: standing: Frank, Edith, Herbert, Mary, Ruth, Percy, May; seated: William Butler snr., William Northcroft Butler, Sarah Jane; front: Lucy, Philip and Muriel.

The circumstances in which Graham Porter and Edith Butler were introduced illustrates the nature of Brethren society. Their meeting did not come about by chance. In the spring of 1908 Edith's parents had toured the Cotswolds in their pony and trap, attracted partly by the charms of the landscape and partly by the knowledge that there were Brethren in the area. They visited the Brethren's Meeting Hall in Burford and were invited to tea by Thomas West Porter, one of the most prominent Brethren in the district. At his house at Holwell they met his son Graham, twenty-seven years old, with the prospect of succeeding to his father's tenancy in the near future. The encounter between two farming families, both Brethren, one with an eligible son, the other with a marriageable daughter, was providential. William Butler was invited to come back, bringing Edith with him. Graham was deputed to meet the guests from their train; he remembered that Edith 'was very red in the face'. Seventy years later he was surprised when it was suggested to him that she might have been blushing.

Twelve days later, on Sunday 21 June, he proposed. She accepted the following day. Her parents insisted that the marriage should be postponed for two years, until Edith came of age. Graham's record of their meetings survives. He first went down to Crondall at the beginning of July. This time it was Edith who picked him up from the station – she was a skilful trap driver, though she never learned to drive a car. Graham was back in Crondall early in September and again a month later. Edith stayed at Holwell in November and December 1908 and in January 1909. In February they stayed with Edith's Uncle Arthur and Aunt Minnie Butler at Poole in Dorset and went on to visit Graham's married sister Evelyn, her husband Harold Hindley and their children at Bourton on the Dorset/Somerset/Wiltshire border. Graham was at Crondall for Easter and spent weekends there in May and June.

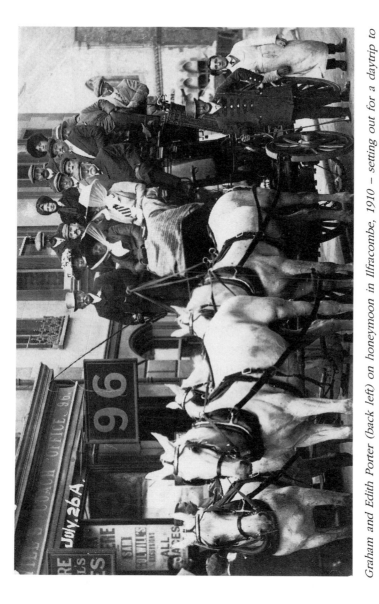

Graham and Edith Porter (back left) on honeymoon in Ilfracombe, 1910 – setting out for a daytrip to Hunters Inn on the Lynton Road.

Edith came to Holwell for a fortnight in July. Although she and Graham saw each other regularly, she visited her future home only once more before their wedding on 20 July 1910. After a honeymoon in the West Country, the newly-weds came back to Manor Farm, Holwell, where Graham 'commenced farming on 29 September – Michaelmas Day – 1910'.

During their engagement Edith and Graham collected together the furnishings they would need to replace those which would follow Graham's father, stepmother and two sisters to Burford where Thomas West Porter planned to live in retirement. Graham's entries in a 'Cooper's Little Red Book', dated 1909, indicate where the items stored at Holwell were bought; the goods which were 'at Crondall' on 12 June 1910 were presented as a single inventory.

The first dated purchase was made in July 1908, a matter of weeks after their engagement. It was a 'dinner service ex-Aunt Craddock's sale' – born in 1831 Mary Craddock was the eldest of Thomas West Porter's four sisters and widow of Robert Craddock of Lyneham, a farmer of 720 acres according to the census of 1881. The incomplete 'Ivy' pattern Wedgwood service cost Graham 13 shillings. The effects they acquired in Oxfordshire came in miscellaneous parcels, for instance, on 2 December 1909 'ex Bartons'.

2 iron saucepans and lids	1s 6d
Glass water jug and 2 bottles	1s 3d
Plated teapot	(no price given)
2 cane seat chairs	2s 6d
Mahogany dressing table	17s 0d
Mahogany toilet glass, marble slab	17s 0d

They came at prices far below those advertised by shops: a new mahogany dressing table would have cost five guineas. Edith and Graham furnished their house from sales. In all their seventy years of married life they hardly bought any new furniture. They passed the habit on to their children: when their youngest son David was setting up home in the 1960s the only item to be purchased new was a three-piece suite costing £75 – a sum which might have been invested in adding another cow to the herd.

Aunt Craddock, c. 1910.

This yeoman thrift was not matched by taste of yeomanly austerity. A Coalport tea service complemented the Wedgwood and, along with the tea service, indeed in the same parcel, came an ormolu cabinet. The 'two skin rugs' which Edith brought with her from Crondall suggest a shared appetite for the occasional exotic touch.

The purchase of a hip bath and hot water cans, a commode, washstands and double and single sets of 'ware' (the suites of jugs and basins, soap dishes, slop buckets and chamberpots), is a reminder of the absence of modern plumbing at Manor Farm. This lack of modern conveniences was typical of the Cotswolds. Mollie Harris's nostalgic tour of *Cotswold Privies,* published in 1984, includes descriptions and photographs of a good number which were still in use. In the 1920s, when Mollie Harris was a child in Ducklington, her family's privy was

> . . . a vault type, the sort that almost everyone in the village had. It was a huge deep hole in the ground and over this was built a box-like contraption with two holes or places to sit. This was a 'two-holer', but some families had three- or four-holers. In ours was a large hole for grown-ups and a smaller one for children, which was set almost a foot lower than the grown-up one, so that the young child could sit on it with ease. It was rather a nice arrangement really – mother and child could sit there at the same time, and the child could learn what to do. The holes should have had wooden lids on when not in use, but not ours; they had most likely gone up the copper hole years ago to help boil the washing up . . .
>
> Twice a year . . . a man came with what we children called the 'lavender cart' . . . we were fascinated to see

him ladling the contents of our vault out with what looked like a very big spoon on the end of a long pole.

At Holwell there were several privies in the garden – some for the family, including a triple one (two large and one small, side by side), and the rest for the servants. The upstairs water closet flushed into a bucket which was emptied from outside. This little room was reached by a dark passage, which in later years Edith's sisters remembered as a 'chamber of horrors'.

The ancient Manor Farm house presented a striking contrast to the Victorian house where Edith had been brought up – when she told her grandchildren stories about her childhood she was keen to point out that Penn Croft had had a bathroom before 10 Downing Street. An entry in Graham's account book for 1916 indicates that Edith inspired some modernization at Holwell: a note under 'rent' reads '14s extra charged, being 5% interest on the cost of hot water supply to the house'. Graham's account books itemise Household Expenses from January 1914. They suggest that he and Edith earmarked modest sums to make the house more comfortable and convenient: lino; a bedstead and mattress; a carpet, a mat and a toilet mirror and a kitchen table were purchased in 1914; more lino in January 1916; a wardrobe, a bedstead and mattress and a pair of vases in November; in June 1917 another wardrobe, a towel horse, a 'cane lounge' and a vase; in January 1918 a mahogany wardrobe, a commode and three chairs. The 'tapestry' bought from Williamson and Cole in May 1919 and in January 1920 was probably intended for curtains or loose covers.

The first of Graham and Edith's children, Graham (known as Frank), was born in the prodigiously hot August of 1911: on the 9th, four days before his birth, the official temperature recorded at

Greenwich was 100 degrees Fahrenheit. He was a bonny baby right from the start. Like his brothers and sisters, he was born at home. Their father's account book notes the fees paid to the doctor who was in attendance and the nurse who supported Edith in the early weeks of her babies' lives – in 1918 Nurse received eight guineas. Graham used to recall how he had to race to Burford on his horse to call the doctor – there was no telephone at Manor Farm in those days. William Basil, Basil to the family, was born on 4 January 1913 ('rainy all day', according to his grandfather's diary). Dorothy Edith was born in 1915, Edna May at the beginning of 1918 and John Humphrey at the end of 1919. (Thomas) Alan, the last member of the family to be born in the Cotswolds, arrived in June 1921, just three months before Graham and Edith moved with their children to Hampshire. Three more children were Hampshire-born: (Margaret) Jean in 1924, Rachel May in 1926 and David Lane in 1934.

Graham and Edith with Basil, Dorothy and Frank, 1916.

Graham's account books contain periodic entries for doctor's bills for visits and prescriptions, usually settled by the year and never itemised. The burden of medical expenses was a consideration in the calculation of parents who opted for small families.

A little bundle of letters which Sarah Jane Butler sent her daughter Edith in the first two months of 1913 offer us a glimpse of her in her role as mother and grandparent. At the beginning of February Basil was four weeks old; Frank was with the Butlers at Crondall. 'Frankie' was, she reported reassuringly, 'quite happy' and at eighteen months, talked 'more than ever'. He was teething and she had given him some 'chammomilla' which had evidently done the trick: 'he is eating very well and sleeping too . . . He came into us this morning quite early, had fine fun with Grandpa'. News from Holwell was worrying, however.

> We are so grieved to hear the precious baby is so poorly. Don't worry dear, for if he is organically strong, I cannot think it can be very serious. Wind causes the poor little things a lot of trouble, for weeks sometimes. Does he cry much? Do you remember how Muriel[41] cried, and what trouble she was for weeks? Have you to wean him and give him different food[42] or diet yourself differently? I am so sorry for you dear, but we can look to Him who does sustain and count upon Him. 'His ways are perfect.'

---

[41] Edith's eight-year-old sister.

[42] Bottle feed him.

129

By the end of the month Frank was back at Manor Farm and Basil was doing better.

> My dearest Edith [her mother wrote from Poole] I was very pleased to get your letter second post with such a detailed account of the dear baby. It was just what I wanted, to know all about him. So thankful Doctor thinks him better. Do hope he will pick up. Should think so now the digestion is better . . . No snow here, but father said they had over one inch at home. Been for three motor drives, it is rather too cold though. Hope Frankie is keeping well this cold weather. I think Graham should drink some hot milk, he is so thin. I know he does not care about it. Are you taking it, good for brain as well as body? . . .
>
> I do not look for a letter so often, dear, just a card to hear how baby is. Will send you a line again or wire tomorrow.
>
> Much love to you both and kisses for Frankie . . .
> Your loving mother

Edith kept these letters because they were the last she received from her mother. In the Porter family, letters, which preserved characteristic phrases and sentiments in a familiar hand, were a favoured, unostentatious way of keeping the memory of a dead parent, partner or child fresh. Their most agreeable grandparental duty done, William and Sarah Jane had gone down to Poole to stay with Arthur and Minnie; his brother had married her sister, not an unusual pattern in Victorian England.

Frank and Basil before they were breeched, c. 1914.

Sarah Jane had not been well, perhaps they hoped that the change of air would do her good. On 4 March William Butler wrote to let the family at Holwell know that

131

Dear Mother is seriously ill. We had two doctors yesterday and they say it is appendicitis – a small abcess near the appendix but not in a bad form – and recommend an operation this afternoon. We are having a physician from Bournemouth this morning, – and if he thinks it right, D.V.' will operate this afternoon. Will send you a line again or wire tomorrow.

She had a very comfortable night last night. Our eyes and hearts are up to God, who is able to carry her safely through. Pray.

I had expected to return home today, but must stay here two or three days now, so have wired to them. Sorry to trouble you, with your present care, but knew you would like to know.

With our love to you all,

Your affectionate Father

She does enjoy 'The Everlasting Arms'. How blessed at times like this, indeed at all times, to know the love that is in Christ Jesus. The two doctors did not come till late last evening or I would have written yesterday. She seemed better but for feverishness, which was the bad symptom.

Sarah Jane died a week later and was buried in Crondall churchyard on 14 March 1913, exactly seventy years to the day before her son-in-law Graham was laid to rest in the same place.

What a sad time it was for poor Edith; only three months later she suffered the loss of her sister-in-law Marian. And yet her Christian faith never wavered and she remained throughout her life a strong support for her husband. One of her favourite verses summed up her philiosophy:

> He knows, He loves, He cares,
> Nothing this truth can dim.
> He does the very best for those
> Who leave the choice to Him.

Edith's father-in-law, Thomas, recorded all these sad events in his pocket diary, including the death of his sister whom he referred to as 'Aunt Craddock'. He noted other family matters, including his visit to an eminent medical consultant, Sir William Ostler, which led to a series of X-Rays and a new course of treatment under the supervision of the Burford physician, Dr Cheatle. Thomas and his second wife Ann had moved with Lizzie and Edie to East View in Burford when Graham and Edith took up residence at Manor Farm. The house fronted on to the road but at the back there was a large garden: he had enough grass to make hay for the horse which was kept in a stable further down the street. As he got older Thomas rode a tricycle as well as driving a pony and trap, especially when he took his wife out. He would also hire a car and driver for long journeys. One curious feature of the garden at East View was the stone quarry, which was crossed by a pretty rustic bridge.

Things which we now take for granted were worth commenting on then: on 17 February 1913 he noted that an aeroplane flew overhead and, later in the year, that one took off from Burford; and in June 1914 he took his brother John and his wife Ellen to see the Wireless Telegraphy poles at Langley.

Top, *East View, High Street, Burford.* Below, *garden of East View, Thomas West Porter with grandchildren – Kathleen, Douglas and Eustace Hindley.*

Sarah Jane's death did not weaken the links with Crondall. Contact was frequent – Edith's father, her brother Frank and their little sister Muriel were often at Holwell. Thomas West Porter noted in his tiny 'waistcoat pocket diary' for 5 February 1914:

> Mild and dry. Frank and Muriel Butler and Edith and Children called . . .

The following day he

> Shot hares Holwell. Mr Butler[43], Baggs and Charlie Bodman into p.m.[44] Frank Butler shot by Gerald . . .

Fortunately, it seems that Frank was 'peppered' rather than badly hurt. In the early years of his sister's marriage, Frank Butler was often at Holwell, helping out at Manor Farm – in 1915 he was recruited as a member of a Cricket XI playing under the colours of Graham Lane Porter's landlord, Squire Fox of the Bradwell Grove Estate.

It was through his father-in-law, no doubt keen to make it easier for him to take Edith and the children down to Penn Croft, that Graham acquired his first car. (Gerald had bought a Model T Ford with a brass radiator at the beginning of 1914.) On and off the farm, Graham was an enthusiast for new technology and remained so for the rest of his life. He rode a horse around the farm but from 1913 he had a Wolf motorcycle for journeys further afield. Norman James, who was born at Holwell in 1907, remembered the 'motor-bike with no clutch, he ran

---

[43] William Northcroft Butler always appears as 'Mr Butler' in the diary.

[44] Prayer Meeting.

and pushed it until it started and then jumped into the saddle'. (The Wolf cost Graham the sight of his left eye: a piece of grit got into it and caused the cornea to ulcerate. In the early days he wore a black patch to protect his blind eye.)

Graham had long had a push-bike. His first had pedals which had to be pushed down (rather than round and round), which he found difficult because his legs were not long enough to reach the bottom of the thrust. Graham had a vivid memory of the first time he saw a bicycle freewheeling – it was on the seafront at Eastbourne: he was amazed to see a rider going along without moving his legs.

Graham's first car, driven to Holwell by his brother-in-law Frank in the spring of 1916, was a year old 15-20 horse power, four-cylinder Studebaker, the lighter of the two-car stable Studebaker offered from 1914. (With the English automobile industry engaged in warwork, American manufacturers made inroads into the English civilian market.) The March 1915 edition of *The Autocar* included 'The Impressions of a Trial Run' for the six-cylinder model, the 15-20 h.p. Studebaker's big-brother:

> Our trial trip proved successful in every way. The engine started up instantly when the electric starter was thrown into action, the sad memories of heavy and exhausting cranking in the past standing out in significant contrast.
>
> The gear changes required only the merest pressure with the palm of the hand against the knob of the level, and each speed snicked into its place with absolute quietude. The acceleration of the car was almost instantaneous. It gets away from the rest like an arrow from a bow and on the level rapidly accelerates up to

three times the legal limit, if it is allowed to do so. It settles down to its work and takes the road at speed like a North-Western express . . . The steering is as light as a feather; while the brakes are powerful but smooth in action.

Among satisfied puchasers in the spring of 1915 was 'Mr F. T. Jane, the well-known authority on naval matters', and publisher of *Jane's Fighting Ships*.

The Studebaker cost Graham £184, plus £7 16s to have it painted, varnished and overhauled. A year later he had the car fitted with electric lamps which, with three bulbs cost him 12s 9d. The insurance with the Ocean Accident Company cost £8 15s; the car licence £6 6s, and registration with Surrey County Council £1. Graham's driving licence cost him 5s a year. It is still in the family's possession along with all the others he had in a driving career which ended only when he was a few months short of a hundred. In all the sixty-six years he had just one brush with the authorities, an endorsement and fine of £3 in 1947 for driving without due care and attention.

As farmers, the last Cotswold generations of the Porter family were not called up to serve in the Great War. Farming was, and long had been, considered an occupation of national importance in war-time, and indeed there is no record of any member of the Porter family ever going to war.

Staccato entries in Thomas West Porter's diary mark the outbreak and early progress of the Great War.

31 July   War between Austria and Servia

```
AUGUST, 1914.                          AUGUST, 1914.

3 MON. Bank Holiday. Dry + cool        6 THUR.        Slight storms
Gerald drove J.H.R. Miss                        O 0.41 a.m.
Drew + I to Cirencester                War with Germany
Fellowship meeting                     Mr + Mr. Rochester also
War news serious                       J.H.R. called

4 TUES. Fine but cloudy                 7 FRI. Dry all day
Mr Reynolds called to                  Wrote E.H.C.
Mr Rochester                           British cruiser sunk
Lizzie home from Banbury               130 lives lost
War news serious
                                              Very wet morning
5 WED. Heavy rain                      8 SAT. S.R. 4.34, S.S. 7.36
Prayer meeting instead                 Mr + Mr Rapson Johnsons
of reading                             Graham to tea
Mr Banle + Mr young called +           J.H.R. + Mr Rochester to
                                       prayer after
```

Then on Bank Holiday Monday,

> 3 August   Dry and Cool . . . War news serious
>
> 4 August   Fine but cloudy . . . <u>War news serious</u>
>
> 6 August   Slight storms. <u>War with Germany</u> . . .
>
> 7 August   Dry all day . . . British cruiser sunk 130 lives lost.
>   Next day he bought a 'War special' for 6d.
>
> 13 August   Very Warm. Battle of Herlem[45]. Germans
>   Repulsed

He bought a 'War Circular' on 16 September and on Sunday 11 October, a 'fine day', noted: 'Antwerp taken by Germans'.

Summing up the year at the end of the diary in the spaces provided for 1 and 2 January 1915 he wrote:

---

[45] Thomas struggled with the spelling of the unfamiliar place name.

The past year has been an eventful one. War broke out early in August, which is still raging with but little prospect of ending as we see, but God is over all and will doubtless turn all to His glory.

His comment on 1916 was:

Another year has closed and what a year! War continues through its whole course and at present no prospect of ending but God knows when. On His part it has been a year of goodness for which we praise Him.

Now seventy-two, Thomas had lost interest in the detailed narrative of war. Only a local casualty warranted notice:

8 January   . . . G. Bishop killed.

The Brethren and family apart, seasonal events dominate his daily record of the last complete year of his life:

4 January   . . . Shot hares at Holwell.
5 January   . . . First aconite out.
14 January   . . . Fox through garden.
17 January   . . . Plum tree blown down last night.

5 April   . . . No drilling done till now.

8 September   . . . Beautiful harvest day. All hands busy.

During September Thomas was busy in the garden, helping to move furniture, walking, picking apples and pears, visiting friends and family and attending meetings as usual. He made the last entry in his diary on Saturday 6 October 1917.

Cold and dry. Move wire in orchard and plant strawberries

On Sunday 7 October as Lizzie, his daughter, recorded in soft pencil in her waistcoat pocket diary:

Very wet in morning. Graham and father went to Stow. Father fell asleep to wake with Christ.

Three days later,

Fine day but even[ing]. Dear father's body laid to rest. Much sustained and comforted.

Thomas West Porter was singing a hymn when he died at a Sunday afternoon Bible study meeting at Stow-on-the Wold. The hymn was printed on the memorial card sent to his family and friends. It ended, fittingly:

To shed no tears, to feel no pain, But see Thee face to face.

Graham was with him and realised immediately that he had 'passed into those eternal joys he had ben singing about'. His body was brought back to Burford and laid to rest in the burial ground next to

If such the happy midnight song,
　　Our prisoned spirits raise,
What are the joys that cause, ere long,
　　Eternal bursts of praise ;

To look within and see no stain,
　　Abroad no curse to trace ;
To shed no tears, to feel no pain,
　　But see Thee face to face.

In Loving Memory

OF

THOMAS WEST PORTER,

(OF BURFORD,)

Who fell asleep, October 7th, 1917,

AGED 73 YEARS.

"Father, I will that they also, whom Thou hast given me, be with me where I am."—*John* xvii, 24.

Thomas West Porter's memorial card.

141

the Baptist Chapel. The Brethren had bought part of this ground and Thomas was the first member of the family to be buried in it. In due course, his second wife Ann, his daughter Edith, his brother John and John's wife Ellen were also laid to rest there.

Thomas had made his will a few weeks after his retirement, on 12 November 1910. It was proved on 24 January 1918. His estate amounted to £8143 10s 9d. It consisted of his house at Burford, a cluster of adjacent properties, money in the bank and a portfolio of shares. His investments are a reminder of the age through which he had lived. Victorian engineers, pre-eminent among them Albert Brassey, whose son and namesake was a local landowner, had built railways across five continents. Thomas had shares in the Canadian Pacific Railway, the Toronto Suburban Railway, the Buenos Aires Great Southern Railway Company, the Grand Trunk Pacific Railway Company, the Antofagasta and Bouria Railway Company, the Calcutta Tramways and the Cunard Steam-ship Company. During his lifetime young Englishmen had gone 'out East' to manage tea and, later, rubber plantations. Thomas had shares in the Jokai Tea Company and the Jonghandor Rubber Estates.

By contrast, his bequests, though couched in convoluted lawyers' language which would have been unfamiliar to his yeomen ancestors of the eighteenth century, apply the same principles which had guided them in the disposal of their earthly goods.

His widow and disabled daughter Edith Susanna were singled out for special consideration. Ann was left his 'furniture, plate, glass, linen, clocks, china, pictures and other household effects . . . during her life' together with a life interest in £2000 and a life tenancy in his dwelling house at Burford. The rents of 'the dwelling house and appurtenances late in the occupation of James Bryan' adjoining 'his house' on the

142

north and 'the three cottages with their appurtenances' to the south were to be used to keep all five dwellings 'in good structural repair'.

Edith, who was disabled by Down's Syndrome, was left a life interest in £1000. If she survived her stepmother (which she did), a further £1000 would revert to her, for her lifetime.

Thomas West Porter's other surviving children, his sons Gerald and Graham Lane and his daughters Evelyn Mary and Eliza Anne (Lizzie) were left equal shares of the residue of his estate. They were, however, required 'to bring into hotchpot and account for' the sums their father had 'advanced' to them: £850 to Gerald, £800 to Graham, £400 to their sister Evelyn. Gerald and Graham's 'advances' had helped to set them up as farmers on their own account; Evelyn's was a contribution to setting up her married home. As the receipts stuck into his account book demonstrate, Graham had repaid his advance before his father's death.

Thomas West Porter was typical in his failure to acknowledge or reward Lizzie's special contribution as the daughter who sacrificed the chance of a home and husband of her own to care for Edith and support her father and stepmother as they got older. Before the Great War the assumption that what the Victorians called 'home duties' should take absolute priority was universal. There is no evidence that any young woman of this or any earlier generation of the Porter family considered taking on paid work outside the family.

On 3 February 1914 Thomas West Porter had added a codicil to his will recording bequests to six of his old employees: John Winfield, 'my late shepherd'; Edward Launchbury, 'my late carter'; Stephen Brunsdon; Caleb Matthews; George Legg and Richard Preston. Shepherd Winfield had come to Holwell in 1872. Caleb Matthews and Stephen Brunsdon, too, had been employed even earlier on lads' wages. These legacies – £15 to the first five named, £5 to Richard Preston – represented substantial sums of money at a time when in low-waged Oxfordshire an agricultural labourer earned around 15 shillings a week. They were also, and perhaps more importantly, tokens of the mutual regard which seems to have characterised the long lasting relationships between the master and the men at Manor Farm in Thomas West Porter's time. In this respect, as in so many others, times were changing. The Great War undermined the traditional equation of farmers' paternalism and workers' deference.

The War had forced farmers to weigh the wage and other costs of horse husbandry against tractors. Some, like Graham Lane Porter, had come down in favour of mechanisation. The younger men, whether they went to war or stayed on the land, had had their eyes opened to the differentials between their wages and those, to look no further, of the 'Tommy' released by the army to bring the harvest home. Perhaps it is little wonder that when Graham was asked about the impact of the First World War on his way of life, he replied: 'The servants weren't

nearly as respectful as they had been.'

From the perspective of the family at Manor Farm, Thomas West Porter's death in 1917 was probably the most momentous event of the war years, loosening the ties that bound Graham to Holwell and the Cotswolds, and counterbalancing the tug of new family links with Hampshire.

David Lane Porter, aged about two, 1937.

144

Graham and Edith Porter with eight of their nine children in 1927. Standing left to right: Edna, Basil, Frank, Dorothy. Seated left to right: Alan, Jean, Rachel and John, with Rupert the spaniel.

Part Three

OXFORDSHIRE

Chapter Seven

THE SQUIRE

homas West Porter had already committed himself to the annual tenancy of Manor Farm at Holwell in Oxfordshire when the Bradwell Grove Estate came on the market in 1871.

Messrs Farebrother, Clark and Co, the London agents who handled the sale advertised the estate thus:

A Valuable Freehold Manorial Domain . . . situated ten miles from Faringdon, six and a half from Lechlade, two from Burford, and three miles from the contemplated station at Alvescott, on the East Gloucester Railway, distinguished as the Bradwell Grove Estate in the parishes of Bradwell, Filkins, Broughton, Kencott, Holwell, Bampton and Shilton in the counties of Oxford and Berks, comprising a capital mansion, seated in a fine park studded with noble Forest and other Trees, and being of considerable Architectural Pretensions, and containing every convenience and accommodation for a family of Distinction; with spacious offices; also suitable lawns, Pleasure Grounds, and a Walled Garden, with Green-houses, Graperies and Arboreta, containing the choicest Specimens of Foreign and other Trees; also Most

149

Extensive Plantations and Woods, through which are Rides and Drives of many Miles, communicating partly by Arches under the Public Roads; Numerous Farms, with Substantial Farm Residences and Numerous Cottages, including the Entire Village of Holwell (Except the Glebe and School House): Also certain Leasehold Properties important as adjuncts to the foregoing. The whole comprises an area of about 3690 Acres, together with the Next Presentation to the Living of Holwell

The Mansion, dating from 1804, was

. . . stone built and castellated, with porch entrance and comprises, on the Upper Floor, A Principal Bedchamber, 21ft by 21ft 6, with Dressing Room adjoining; another Principal Bedchamber nearly similar size to the preceding, also with Dressing Room; Eight good Secondary Bed Rooms, Nursery, Bath Room, Housemaid's Closet, Linen Closet and Two Water Closets. On the Ground Floor, Entrance Hall or Vestibule with Groined Ceiling and fireplace; Inner Hall (with Groined Ceiling), from which rises a Noble Stone Staircase, with Oak Handrail and Iron Balustrade, well lighted (Window partly Stained Glass) and Secondary Staircases; Dining Room 31ft by 21ft, Exclusive of Recess, walls painted green and finished with Marble Chimney Piece; Drawing Room, 31ft by 21 ft, elegantly papered, with Three Windows overlooking the Grounds. Communicating with the Drawing Room is a Billiard Room, which opens into the Conservatory or

Orangery 43ft by 15ft. On the right of the Hall is a Corridor which leads to the Ladies Boudoir. On the floor are also a Study (with Concealed Staircase communicating with the first floor) and small Room adjoining, Plate Closet, Store Room, Housekeeper's Room, Servant's Hall, Butler's Pantry and Bed Room opposite, Brushing Room, Butler's Room, Still Room, Kitchen, Scullery, Cook's Pantry or First Larder, Second Larder, and Two Bed Rooms over Kitchen with Separate Staircase. And excellent Ale, Beer, and Wine Cellars in the Basement.

The document goes on to detail how the walls of the large kitchen garden were 'clothed with choice fruit trees'; there was a 'peach house and vinery' and a melon ground. The Arboretum was distinguished by 'fully grown specimens of Wellingtonia Gigantea, Arbutus, Pinus Insignis and Excelsa, Cedar, Argenta, Deodara, Leboni etc and many varieties of Flowering Shrubs'.

'The Noble Park' in which the Mansion stood was 'studded with Forest and other Trees'. Among the park's specified attractions were pheasant pens. And, it was emphasised, 'The Heythrop and old Berkshire and Vale of White Horse packs Hunt the District; the Heythrop Pack meet in the Park once a month.

'The Mansions, Gardens and Pleasure Grounds' had recently been 'let furnished to Victor B. Van der Weyer, Esq. for a term' which would expire on Christmas Day 1871. Van der Weyer's presence was a bonus for agents and purchaser alike. An old Etonian, married in 1868 to the daughter of an earl, Van der Weyer was a prominent member of county society in late-Victorian Berkshire, Colonel of the Berkshire Militia and High Sheriff of the County in 1885.

The description is worth quoting at length not simply for the luxuriance of its phraseology but because the expansive prose was calculated to entice just such a man as rose to the bait.

In 1871 the purchase of a mansion set in an estate of 3690 acres was still a prospect to fire the imagination of the *nouveaux riches*. As Trollope's Archdeacon Grantly pointed out to his son in *The Last Chronicle of Barsetshire,* published in 1867, 'Land gives you so much more than rent. It gives you a position and influence and political power, to say nothing about the game.'

About this time, Albert Brassey, son and namesake of the contractor responsible for constructing railways in Argentina, Australia, Canada, the Crimea, France, India, Italy and Moldavia, acquired the Heythrop estate, not far from Bradwell Grove, and commissioned the eminent architect Alfred Waterhouse to design a replacement for the early eighteenth-century house which had been damaged by fire in 1831. Waterhouse worked on his plans for over a year, only to find that Brassey had changed his mind in favour of restoring the burned-out shell.

The Bradwell Grove Estate was bought by William Henry Fox, son of a Yorkshire manufacturer. (Most of these would-be country gentlemen were inheritors rather than originators of industrial fortunes; founding a firm was an all-consuming business.) Folk memory has Samuel Fox, William Henry's father, down as a manufacturer of crinolines who turned to umbrella-making as the fashion for hoops faded. Sadly, the chronology of the crinoline tells against the story. Fox was making ribs for umbrellas by 1848 while, as late as 1863, the year of Samuel Fox's death, *Punch* was still poking fun at the housemaids who, banned from wearing their hoops because they sent crockery crashing to the ground, felt undressed and unequal to opening the door – even to the chimney sweep – without their crinolines on.

Fox's original products were more mundane: fishhooks and the pins used for carding wool. When he diversified into umbrella ribs Fox produced the first satisfactory steel rib. Then he refined it. By 1853 his factory in Stocksbridge near Sheffield was producing ribs which were, in the words of the firm's Centenary History, 'in all essential details the prototype of the ribs used in umbrellas today'. The Fox umbrellas' reputation rested on an ingenious but simple machine, devised in 1853 and still in use the best part of a century later. It flexed the ribs, breaking those 'which are too hard' and kinking 'the ribs which are too soft' so that they could 'easily be distinguished and rejected'.

William Henry, Squire Fox of Bradwell Grove as he liked to be known, took to his new role with relish, while maintaining a proper pride in the foundations of his fortune – new staff received a Fox umbrella to mark their first Christmas at the house. The bachelor Fox and his widowed mother lived in style. According to Norman James, the indoor staff at Bradwell Grove consisted of

> . . . a butler, two footmen, a housekeeper, three kitchen maids, two scullery maids, one dairy maid, four housemaids, one seamstress, a hall boy, a lamp man and one boiler man. Outdoors there was a stud groom, four tackmen and two coachmen for a string of about ten horses and coach horses. There were ten gardeners, five gamekeepers, five woodmen, one building foreman, four masons, three carpenters, one cabinet maker, an engineer driver for the portable engine, and lodge-keepers at the gates.

The census returns of 1881 and 1891 record a family of three – on each occasion Mrs Fox and her son were entertaining a visitor, Miss Anna or Annie Young, a couple of years William Henry's junior – with a resident indoor staff of twelve or thirteen (they were between butlers in 1891): housekeeper, lady's maid, cook, a trio of housemaids, a kitchenmaid, a dairymaid and a scullerymaid; an 'odd man' and two footmen.

Fox liked to play the part of a country gentleman, stern yet kindly. On Sunday morning, Norman James remembered, 'Mr Fox would take note of those who were absent from church: You had to have a good reason for not going.' But he met 'all church expenses' and tipped the choir a gold sovereign at Christmas.

> The Christmas Tree party was always held in the Servants Hall, with cake, jellies, fruit and sweets served by the staff, followed by a trip to the Boot Room for the tree lit with candles and surrounded by parcels and toys galore. Before the presents were given, the children always sung 'D'ye Ken John Peel', Mr Fox's favourite song.

The choice of song is revealing. Mr Fox assumed the role of sporting Squire. The sale particulars of 1871 had stressed that the estate was in the Heythrop country, indeed the historian of the Heythrop hunt considered 'the vicinity of Bradwell Grove the beau ideal of a stone-walled county'. In 1921 the sales particulars added the statistic for the average kill of game birds in the five years leading up to the Great War: 2053 pheasants, 908 partridges and 766 hares. But the fox was Mr Fox's favourite prey.

Mr Brassey of Heythrop was Master of the Heythrop Fox Hounds for forty-five years from 1873. In keeping with the ample style these newcomers adopted he met all their expenses, at a time when 'the cost of hunting a country . . . was generally estimated at £1000 for every day in the week that the hounds hunted'. Fox could not compare with 'the king of Heythropshire' – J. P., Commander of the Oxfordshire Yeomanry, High Sheriff of the County, Director of the Great Western Railway, but G. T. Hutchinson's history of the hunt records the 'Squire's' moment of glory when one of his foxes provided a memorable run at the start of Charles Sturman's first season as Huntsman:

> In 1901 fog had stopped hunting at the opening meet at Heythrop, and on Wednesday 4th of November hounds met at Bradwell Grove. Needless to say 'Squire'[46] Fox gave a warm welcome to the new huntsman and begged him to kill one of his foxes as soon as possible.
>
> No sooner said than done. The bitches found at once in the big wood, ran a left hand ring round Shilton, and swung back over the road leading from Burford to Bradwell Grove. From this point they raced past Holwell through Jolley's Gorse[47] to Bibury old race course, where they crossed the Aldsworth road for Sherborne Park leaving Blackpits on the left. The fox crossed Sherborne to Sandpits, but was so beat that he could not get over the wall, so turned down to the Duckery where the bitches caught him at the gate.

---

[46] The quotation marks which qualify 'Squire' are Hutchinson's.

[47] A famous covert.

Buying into Oxfordshire society in the 1870s, Mr Brassey and 'Squire' Fox belong to the penultimate generation to convert industrial wealth into agricultural domains. They proved a poor financial investment. At the end of the decade English agriculture was afflicted by a profound depression from which it did not emerge until the twentieth century. As the *Estates Gazette* explained in June 1892,

> Men who have made money in business and by judicious investment are getting 3½ to 4½ per cent per annum on their spare capital and seem now but little disposed to take on themselves the ownership of land to get only at best a return of 2½ per cent.

For years on end 'Glorious domains and stately homes' were offered in vain. Oscar Wilde speaking through Lady Bracknell put it pithily:

> . . . land ceased to be either a profit or a pleasure. It gives one position and prevents one from keeping it up.

To leave his lasting mark on the village, Squire Fox had a new church built in 1894. This replaced one which had been built less than fifty years earlier to replace a much older chapel. In his petition to the Bishop for permission to erect the new building, Fox referred to the old one as being structurally unsafe and incapable of substantial repair, but it took nearly as long to pull down the 1840s church as it did to build the new one. Fox was shielded from the effect of the depression by dividends from the Stocksbridge factory. His young tenant Thomas West Porter was not, of course, feather-bedded in this way.

Chapter Eight

PROMISE & DISASTER

he records of Thomas West Porter's farming career begin in 1870 when he crossed the county boundary from Gloucestershire to become a tenant on the Bradwell Grove Estate in Oxfordshire. He saw two harvests in at Bradwell Home Farm before he moved across the estate to Manor Farm, Holwell, which he worked until his retirement in 1910. The soil was the same as in his home village of Great Barrington and, in the 1860s, the management of the Heythrop Hunt had decreed that Bradwell Grove was 'to be considered either an Oxfordshire or a Gloucestershire fixture, at the discretion of the master.'

The sales catalogue for the Bradwell Grove Estate described Manor Farm thus:

Situate in the Parish of Holwell with the Manor of Holwell comprising The Manor House being a Comfortable Residence, containing in the attic – two rooms. FIRST FLOOR – five Bed and Dressing Rooms, Water Closet, Store Room suitable for School Room, China Closet, Principal and Secondary Staircases. GROUND FLOOR – Entrance Hall; Dining Room; Drawing Room, finished with Marble Chimney Piece, and Windows overlooking the

Grounds, Kitchen, Back Kitchen, Pantry and Dairy. BASEMENT – Cellar.

PLEASURE GROUNDS, Very tastefully laid out with Walks and Parterres of Flowers, Summer-house and Flower Garden. Kitchen Garden, Abundantly Stocked with Wall and other Fruit Trees.

Large Orchard in the Rear of the Residence, Drying Ground, and Timber Yard. The Outbuildings most conveniently placed, Comprise Brew House, Fowl House, Wood House, Meal House, Potato House, Carpenter's Shop, Wood Shed, Two yards with Horse Sheds, Lime House and Loft over with Wool Room, Piggeries, Two Nag Stables, Two Coach Houses, Two Enclosed Yards with Horse Sheds and Loose Box, Double Barn, Chaff House, Implement Shed, Machine House, Poultry House, Stable for Nine Horses with Loft over, Cart Shed and Granary over. Across the Road is Cart Shed and Granary over.

Detached in No 74 on Plan are Two Barns, yard with Chaff House, Root House, Cattle Shed and Well, another yard with Pump; Two Sheds for Cattle, Pig yard with Sheds.

The names of the fields followed: Church Ground, Thirts Field and Pond, Two Bush Ground, Great Timbers (or Tumblers) Ground, Picket Ground, Coleway (or Cotaway) Ground, Great Clay Furlong, Little Clay Furlong, Hill Sides, Walnut Tree and Ewe Pen Close, The Green, Farther Green, Grove Ground, Ryal's Ground, Long Ground, Broad Close, Close Ends, Long Lands, Old Pits and Glissard's Ground –

altogether 458 acres 2 roods and 6 perches. (At the age of one hundred Thomas West Porter's son Graham could still remember the names of all the fields although he had left the farm sixty years earlier.)

The thirteen cottages and allotment land which went with Manor Farm were occupied by yearly tenants.

Unsurprisingly, the agents stressed the property's farming assets and genteel amenities. When, in his seventies, Thomas West Porter's eldest son Gerald recalled his childhood home, the setting for a bygone way of life, he naturally emphasised the farm's historic characteristics. All the evidence we have suggests that Thomas West Porter was a forward-looking young man. He kept up to date with developments in farming as an annual subscriber to the local Oxfordshire Agricultural Society and to the Royal Agricultural Society of England at the cost of one guinea each.

Farmers' confidence was high when Thomas West Porter started his career. Between 1760 and 1860 the population had more than doubled. Farmers had responded heroically to the challenge of feeding the crowded island: they had increased their output by one hundred per cent. Their reward was handsome, the first forty years of Victoria's reign was their golden age. Looking back on his life as a 'West Country Yeoman' Sam Kendall saw 'that wonderful season of 1874' as 'the zenith' of the golden age, 'attended as it was by a magnificent harvest when corn maintained a fairly remunerative price, whilst the values of beef, mutton, milk, butter, cheese and wool all showed a steady increase . . . Fortunate indeed were those of us in any way connected directly or indirectly with such a prosperous industry'.

Prospects in the sheep and corn country of the Cotswolds were promising: in 1840 the Royal Agricultural Society of England recognised two classes of long wool sheep – Leicester and the rest. In 1876 classes were established for Lincolns and Cotswolds. Thomas West Porter had married into the aristocracy of Cotswold sheep farmers. His wife's kinsmen, the Lanes and the Garnes, were among the premier exponents of the breed.

At Michaelmas 1871, the traditional late September beginning of the farming year, Thomas West Porter listed the men and boys he had hired to work Manor Farm: Alfred Moss, carter; George Johnson, shepherd; Henry Calcutt, oxman; John and William Calcutt, ploughboys; Stephen Brunsdon, odd boy; James Buckingham, ploughboy; Caleb Matthews, second carter; Selim Matthews, under shepherd; Zekiel Matthews, ploughboy; Edward Paintin, third carter; Charles Brodrick, odd boy; and Mary Claridge, general servant. With four more men he 'agreed' premiums 'more than other men': W. Brunsdon, groom; H. Hopes, gardener; P. Matthews, 'to feed tegs'; and J. Brodrick.

The men who were 'hired' were guaranteed employment until Michaelmas 1872. Those who were not were 'day men', whose earnings fluctuated with the weather. The presence of a single live-in 'general servant' is a clear indication that Thomas's twenty-eight-year-old wife, Mary Jane, was his active partner, able and willing to cook and keep the house, as farmers' wives had done since the middle of the sixteenth century when Thomas Tusser celebrated their industry and thrift. Almost certainly Mary Jane Porter's knowledge and understanding covered the whole range of Cotswold farming: her mother Sarah Susanna Waine, widowed in 1858, farmed 520 acres in Great Barrington on her own account for well over a decade. The most vivid image we have of Mary Jane before her final illness comes from her son Gerald's description of Manor Farm in his childhood and portrays her as a woman of strength and energy: grasping the old gander which terrorised her children 'by the neck and swinging him round and round, she would let him go sprawling down the yard which was not at all to his ideas of gander dignity'.

'Prize Shearlings at the Royal Agricultural Show, Lewes, Sussex, 1852,' belonging to William Lane. The dust jacket depicts William Lane, the brother of Sarah Susanna Waine, with his shepherd and prize-winning sheep in 1861, when the census showed that he was forty-five years old, married with six children and farming 700 acres at Broadfield Farm, Eastington. He died there, aged ninety-three, in 1908.

(left) Sarah Susanna Waine, the mother of Mary Jane Porter and sister of William Lane.

(below) Jane Lane, née Garne (1776-1875) mother of William Lane and Sarah Susanna Waine. The portrait was painted by the same artist who depicted William Lane's prize-winning sheep.

The list of livestock on the farm on New Year's Day 1872 confirms that corn and sheep were at the core of Thomas West Porter's business. In his first season at Manor Farm he had nine working horses, probably shires or 'agriculturals' as they were often known, eight oxen, 108 breeding ewes and four rams plus a fattening flock. The other cattle and pigs were sidelines. No poultry were listed.

Thomas practised the, by this time, traditional Cotswold rotation of roots, barley, oats, peas, 'seeds' and wheat. The 'seeds' – sainfoin, ryegrass, trefoil, red and white clovers, trifolium and mustard – were fodder crops for the sheep. From the first he supplemented the diet with what he called 'artificial' food – bran, maize and cake. Under John Winfield's management, the sheep were penned all the year round and the input of artificials substantially increased.

In the mid-seventies he invested in manure and chemical fertilisers (nitrate soda in 1875 and superphosphate in 1876) to improve the yield of the 'hungry' but productive stonebrash soil. Throughout the decade Thomas West Porter made significant changes in his farming practice. The last oxen were sold off in 1877: two in February and the remaining four in late August at £26 a head. In 1878 he hired a steam cultivator. From 1873, at least, he had hired steam thrashing tackle in the autumn. These years of promise and innovation came to an end in 1879.

In the late 1870s the golden era of Victorian farming turned to dross. Sam Kendall, whose family farmed in Wiltshire, devoted two chapters of his autobiography, the bleakest of the 'memorial books' of the 1940s, to 'the fateful year of 1879'. He called them 'The Darkest Days of Agriculture' and 'Devastating Ruin'.

Thomas West Porter worked Manor Farm through the deep depression which engulfed English agriculture in the 'fateful year' and persisted for the rest of the century. The old farmers' adage 'have as many strings to your bow as you prudently can' proved ultimately unreliable. A man could no longer be confident that 'if you have it not in the Singing Psalms, you will have it in the Reading Psalms', the recipe tried and tested over many decades. The theory that 'A mixture of sheep farming and husbandry is the best mode of occupying either the richest or the poorest arable land' no longer guaranteed a profit.

The Great Agricultural Depression had twin roots: years on end of cruelly unseasonable weather, and unprecedented and increasing competition from abroad. The repeal of the Corn Laws in 1846 had deprived English farmers of the protection they had enjoyed since 1815 when the government banned the import of foreign wheat until the home grown grain was scarce enough to command high prices. The farmers finally lost a hard-fought campaign to preserve this protectionist regime during the 'Hungry Forties', at the time when famine threatened in Ireland.

Farmers in the Americas and Australasia had far lower costs than their English counterparts. Steam trains and ships created world-wide markets for corn, wool and, as refrigeration came in, meat, butter and cheese. Sam Kendall recognised the benefits these new sources of cheap food conferred on 'workers in the towns and cities' but 'many hundreds of [farming] tenants were out of business' and 'many of their derelict farms could not find tenants'. Mr Brassey's railway contracts, which enabled his son to restore Heythrop in the early 1870s and to continue to subsidise the Heythrop hounds to the tune of £1000 every day they hunted for the next forty-five years, contributed to the diminishing returns of English agriculture. Argentine beef, Canadian wheat, Australian wheat, wool, mutton and beef were transported on Brassey's lines. By the end of Thomas West Porter's farming career, more than half the cereals and a third of the meat consumed in the United Kingdom were imported.

Fashion added to Thomas West Porter's adversity: a new preference for fine wool fabrics eroded the market for the coarse long stapled fleeces of the Cotswold's native sheep. Only the dairyman who specialised in sales of fresh milk was exempt from global competition: the Cotswolds were not suited to dairying on a commercial scale. Larger tenant farmers, men with 150 acres or more, employers of labour like Thomas West Porter, were the worst hit. The plight of men like him with large or growing families was especially anxious.

Thomas West Porter's older neighbour, John Simpson Calvertt, left a graphic account of the great agricultural depression in the eastern Cotswolds. In April 1876, Calvertt, Lincolnshire born and bred, re-established himself, his wife Jane, their six children and '4 tons 16 cwt and 2 qtrs' weight of furniture' on 2483 acres of crown land at Leafield, between Burford and Witney. He was forty-five. Though a farmer on a much bigger scale than Thomas West Porter, he worked similar land – most of it stonebrash – and faced similar difficulties in the bad years of the late nineteenth century. In the golden age commercially-minded men like Calvertt recognised that, as tenants, they could operate on a bigger scale and expect to enjoy greater profits than they could hope for from the acreage they could afford to own. Indeed, it was Calvertt's desire to expand his farming business that led him to emigrate to Oxfordshire.

Outside their shared agricultural concerns Thomas West Porter and John Simpson Calvertt had little in common. Calvertt represents the type of tenant farmer William Cobbett had condemned fifty years earlier as 'mock gentle folks'. Calvertt made regular excursions to London to take in a play and hunted with the Heythrop. In his diary the Bradwell Grove Estate features as the scene of memorable chases. In January 1877, in his first season at Leafield, Calvertt

> . . . met the hounds at Bradwell Grove, ran a ringing fox and lost him – found 2nd in Jolly's Gorse, in which the hounds ran 1¼ hours and killed – found a 3rd and ran to Sherborne Cow pasture – misty day – Mr Price piloted me to Shipton![48]

Thomas West Porter, whose identity and person must have been familiar to Calvertt, from the legend on his farm waggons, from the sale ring and from the annual Hiring Fair at Burford, does not warrant a mention in the text of Calvertt's diary, which was edited by Celia Miller and published by Alan Sutton in 1983. The names Calvertt drops are those of the cream of Cotswold sporting society – the Brasseys feature prominently – together with the Churchills of Blenheim.

Calvertt's annual summings up of the fortunes of the farming year convey the incremental desperation which gripped the agricultural world from the late 1870s:

> 1877 was wet and cold, in the Spring – a hot, short summer – very wet latter Harvest – wet all through November, and rain, snow and wind the last 8 or 9 days of December – bad yielding harvest, thro' frosts in flowering time – very few Apples, scarcely any stone Fruits, no acorns – but abundance of Nuts, only!!!

---

[48] A newcomer to Heythropshire, Calvertt needed an expert guide across country.

The gloomy agricultural scene was matched in other sectors of the economy. 1878 was 'one of the worst on record for Commerce, Trade and Agriculture'. The seasons were out of joint. On 15 April 1879 Calvertt noted:

> Extraordinary morning – 3 inches of snow on the level – such a fall of snow, so late in Spring, has not been seen during my lifetime of nearly 50 years.

It snowed again on May Day. Rain followed. In the middle of June, Calvertt

> . . . could neither plough nor work the land, weed corn – clip sheep. The Country in the worst state I ever knew it in my life. Seasons are ruining English Farmers and Farming.

The harvest season that year was bad:

> . . . the most cursed ruinous weather on record – cannot thrash oats – plough Fallows – skerry (weed) turnips, nor even carry manure on the clover land for wheat!!! – and this state of things has been going on all over the Country since last April!!!

1879 ended with the Tay Bridge disaster, which Calvertt noted with an exaggerated number of casualties.

> . . . the entire train from Edinboro', while crossing the Tay
> Bridge, was carried by 13 spans of Girders to the bottom –
> every Carriage, girder, & c: left no vestige behind of its
> whereabouts – about 100 persons are supposed to have
> perished – not <u>one</u> alive to report the awful catastrophe –
> the most <u>appalling</u> railway accident[49] of this <u>most</u>
> <u>wretched</u> year . . . So ends the most <u>ruinously</u> ugly-
> <u>seasoned</u> year of <u>this century</u>.

The market in land was also hit. On 1 July 1880 the bidding for the
Carbridge Estate '884 acres with Houses, Cottages & Buildings' reached
£20,000, the reserve was £42,000. For Calvertt, sporting prospects
offered some consolation. Grouse were said to be '<u>healthy, strong &</u>
<u>numerous</u>'. But disasters crowded in. On the last day of 1881 Calvertt,
his grasp of international affairs uncertain, recorded:

> Great winds and storms during the past year.
>   The Czar of Russia – blown to pieces; President
> Garfield shot and Earl Beaconsfield [Disraeli] died during
> the past year!!!
>   Agriculture is sadly depressed – more abundant corn
> and Fruit and vegetable crops – but Harvest sadly injured,
> by frequent rains at gathering.

The following year, 1882, he carried the last of his 'harvest Home,
begun 10th August' on 15 November.

---

[49] The most valuable part of the train, the engine, was raised from the bed of the Tay.
Referred to afterwards as 'The Diver', it remained in service until 1919.

Taking Agriculture all round, 1883 was 'the best' he had experienced in Oxfordshire; 1884 was among the 'best years for suitable weather' – farmers welcome sun, rain and frost in due season – but 1885 was 'the most unprofitable year for farming' since Calvertt began his career in 1852, and 1887 was worse. 1889 and 1890 were kind to Calvertt but '1891 and 1892 . . . proved to be the most ruinous of [his] life'. Of 1893 he wrote despairingly, 'of all wretched years in Agriculture, this takes the cake!!!' 1894 was 'a further ruinous year' with wheat prices 'the lowest on record'. 1895 was another

> . . . wretched ruinous year (for owners and occupiers) . . .
> We are fighting the Ashantis, France, the Cubans – Italy,
> the Abyssinians; & Tom Fool Brag, 'President Cleveland'
> will blow us all out of the water – sometime during our
> Future eventful year 1896!

By the end of 1896, 'a gleam of hope' was 'setting in'. The year of the old Queen's Diamond Jubilee was 'a great improvement' and 1898 'very productive'; though the final year of his life, 1899, saw Calvertt less optimistic.

Calvertt's account is confirmed by detached observers. John Orr, who surveyed Oxfordshire farming for the Institute of Research into Agricultural Economics at the University of Oxford in 1914, claimed that

> . . . on the basis of inaccurate analysis of agricultural
> conditions about 1870, extraordinary estimates of what
> agricultural land was worth were made and extraordinary
> prices paid for farms, prices on which an adequate return
> could not be obtained from any production that was
> possible.

Orr cited a farm of 250 acres added to an unnamed estate in 1872. The land cost £95 an acre; the cost of new buildings raised the capital investment to £107; 55s an acre would have been the realistic rent but 24s was all the market would bear even at its height. In 1884 the rent was reduced to 9s an acre, the following year it was down to 8s. Oriel College, a big landowner in Oxfordshire and Berkshire, was forced to cut its tenants' rents by between a quarter and a half.

The cultural and philosophical chasm which separated John Simpson Calvertt and Thomas West Porter is reflected in their response to these desperately hard times. To Thomas West Porter, the unremitting blows were divine retribution. The winter of 1878-79 was one of the coldest of the century. An entry in a notebook primarily devoted to spiritual reflections records that he was 'suffering from a cold with all its depressing attendants. The fields are covered with snow and frosts and have been for some weeks, and my inner feelings have lately seemed to correspond with the outer world'. His entry for 29 August reveals frustration verging on despair:

> Our God in His infinite wisdom and love is at this present time trying our faith severely by sending us continual rains in the very midst of harvest, so that although the corn is nearly all out nothing can be put in the stack. We have tonight been comforted by the 4th of Mark in which we find Jesus rebuking the winds if He sees fit. We do not ask that it shall be so unless it be His will, but we do ask that His grace may be bestowed upon us so that we may be kept from rebelling against His will and from harbouring suspicions of His faithfulness and love.

On 28th December 1879, 'the last Sabbath of another year' he wrote:

> O Lord my heart is filled with grateful emotions tonight that Thou hast mercifully spared me during the past year and, although it was a year of very great trial and I have been many times fain to cry out, 'I know not what to do', yet, blessed be Thy name, O Lord, by Thy grace I have been able to add 'But my eyes are on Thee, O Lord.'

On 13 July 1880 Thomas wrote:

> Gracious God, I acknowledge with a grateful heart the application of Thy word – I awoke this morning, we are in the midst of haymaking, and I wished for fine weather but it is raining in torrents and has done more or less for several days. I thought, whatever can we do if this continues? When the words came into my mind 'Trust the Lord with all thine heart and lean not to thine own understanding. In all thy ways acknowledge Him and He shall direct thy paths.' I prayed for strength to enable me to do so and to keep me from rebelling against the will of my loving Father and I then looked on the almanac for the text for the day and it was this: 'The Lord God omnipotent reigneth'. Will anyone dare to say that it was by chance that this text was marked for today? I know they will but I am convinced that it was the work of the Holy Spirit that, as the Comforter Who has been sent into the world unto us, He applied this word to my heart to comfort and support me in this most trying season.
>
> O, I ask Thee, Heavenly Father, to keep me from

repining and rebelling against Thy will, thankful that Thou knowest all our needs and will not forsake those that trust in Thee.

A second passage from his spiritual notebooks confirms that Thomas West Porter measured his conduct not against the morality of the market place but in the sight of God. It should be noted that the passage was written in a year for which the farm accounts are missing:

December 6th 1882

I would record tonight a circumstance in my experience about which I have been much exercised and which has harassed me a good deal lately, although of a nature connected with carnal things, yet there are certain features in it that may not be unprofitable to note down. It is of the purchase of a mare, which was bought for one sound and healthy but which has proved to be almost worthless. And the deceit practised upon me and the falsehoods uttered and written at the time of buying and in the correspondence over it since are simply shocking to contemplate. And, as a further negotiating with the seller seemed only likely to add lie upon lie, I have refrained from writing to him again. And amongst it all, Satan has been busy in tempting me to harbour feelings of hate and revenge. I trust, however, that the grace of God has in some measure kept down this sin so that I feel no malice towards him now, but pity has taken possession of me and an earnest desire that the Lord may lead him to see the folly of his ways and that he may seek forgiveness where alone it can be found.

Again I have been tempted to deceit and dishonesty myself. Put her into a sale and use what means you can to make her appear sound, has been the suggestion: You may rid yourself of her very well. But, thanks be to God, I have been kept, the thought has come: How can I do this great wickedness to sin against God? And now, Lord, I desire to cast this case upon Thee and look to Thee for future guidance in this matter. Amen.

To Thomas West Porter, in the last resort, 'carnal things' were of negligible importance except as a spiritual education. Temporal adversity was a test of faith.

These spiritual reflections aside, it is the unemphatic entries in his account books which provide the clearest evidence of the financial difficulties Thomas West Porter faced. His Holwell accounts are preserved in two handsome parchment-bound volumes running from 1871 to 1880 and from 1883-84 to June 1889. A few pages at the end of the first volume and many at the beginning of the second have been cut out. The characteristic rulings to bracket the totals at the foot of these pages, just visible on the stubs which remain, indicate that, at some time, the records for all or part of the intervening period have been destroyed.

Like Oriel's tenants, Thomas West Porter had his rents abated by his landlord. Thomas took Manor Farm on at a rent of £662 per annum, £1 9s an acre. In the 'fateful year' of 1879 and in 1880 his rent was reduced by 15%. When the records resume in 1883-84 he was paying £1 5s 4d an acre; in 1884-85, £1 2s 2d and in 1885-86 14s 3 d, roughly half what he had ben paying at the start of his tenancy. In 1886-87, the total rent went up from £327 13s 6d to £530 1s 6d but the recovery was not sustained and in 1887-88 it dropped back to £401 11s 6d. Even with a much-reduced rent bill, the farm did not pay its way. Thomas was forced to dip into his reserves in 1883-84; in 1886-87 he again lost money. In 1887-88, to keep the farm going, he drew on his own savings and investments in his children's names – this money had come to them from their grandmother Sarah Susanna Waine, who died three months before her daughter Mary Jane in February 1885, leaving over £13,000.

There are further indications of the persistent depression. In 1883-84 Thomas West Porter adopted explicit 'rules' for the annual valuation of his stock and crops. Their successive applications indicate a progressive decline in profits from wheat. In 1873 Thomas's total income from grain was in the region of £1470; in 1888 it was £1000 less. From 1872 until 1885 Thomas kept a detailed record of each field's yield; the variety – Golden Drop wheat, for instance, or Scotch Chevalier barley; dates of thrashing – any time from September to the following July; and his verdict 'good' or 'poor'.

In 1884, after a long period of spiritual uncertainty and distress, Thomas West Porter, who had been brought up by his mother Mary Porter to know the New Testament verse by verse and to recognise the hand of God in the incidents of his daily life, left the Church of England for the Exclusive Brethren. On the Bradwell Grove Estate regular attendance at Holwell Church was regarded as a duty to God and the Squire. Although Thomas West Porter's defection was undoubtedly a blow to the proper pride of his landlord, Fox had to weigh his displeasure against more than the simple improbability of finding another satisfactory tenant for Manor Farm. Thomas West Porter was evidently a fair-dealing man and the employer on whom most of the families in Holwell depended. Making life harder for him would increase the hardship of families on the estate whose welfare 'Squire' Fox was expected – not least by his sporting friends – to take to heart. Thomas's tenancy was renewed annually until he retired in 1910.

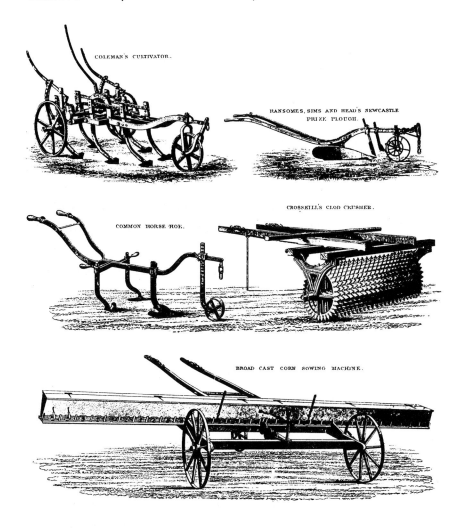

Examples of farm machinery in 1886

Later, at the end of his career at Manor Farm, Thomas West Porter summed up his experience as a Cotswold farmer in a paper headed, 'Some remarks on the Farming of Oxfordshire, written for the Journal of the Oxfordshire Agricultural Society':

> The district of which I am enabled to speak is in the neighbourhood of Burford and lies at the extreme west of the county. It forms a portion of the Cotswold Hills. It is chiefly arable excepting some meadows running beside the river Windrush and around most of the villages there are a few pasture grounds. The woodland is a small proportion, except the forest of Wychwood, and scarcely any waste. The soil generally is a light stonebrash on the oolite formation, well adapted for the breeding and feeding of sheep. The fields are for most part large with stone wall fences.
>
> There have been no material changes within the last twenty years in the reclamation of woodland or waste but just previous to that time there was a considerable quantity of land reclaimed from woodland and forest in the Wychwood forest. Several new farmsteads were erected on the most approved style and farms laid out to them, varying in size from 400 to 1,000 acres. This improvement was effected by the Owner who now lets the farms which have changed hands several times within the time mentioned. There has been no poor pasture land converted to arable but I have noticed a tendency to lay down some of the latter to permanent pasture. However, this is only done to a very small extent nor is it likely to

be as the soil can be made to produce considerably more keep when worked in rotation.

There has been no draining done, in fact there is only a very small percentage of the land that would be at all improved by it. Chalking or marling is never thought of here and with regard to levelling fences, as I said at the commencement, the fields are large therefore few fences to remove. I have, however, removed three miles of hedgerows on the farm within the last seven years. These were standing by the side of walls which in some places have been rebuilt while in other they also have been taken away and new quicks planted.

Speaking of the district generally, there has not been much outlay in improving the farm buildings, which in many places are in a very dilapidated condition. However, there are exceptions – the owner of the Bradwell Grove Estate, for instance, I am pleased to say is improving the buildings on the estate and building some new cottages which were very much needed and, although, of course, the farmer must reap a benefit from any improving in the buildings which his landlord may make, I do not consider it has been carried on sufficiently to make a material difference to the farmers in this district.

The prevailing systems of cropping mostly are the four-field course, i.e. roots, barley, seeds and wheat, but I have noticed that winter beans are planted a great deal more frequently than formerly and, whereas the farmyard manure used to be applied for roots, the latter are now grown generally with only the aid of artificials and the manure is laid on the seeds or on the barley stubble for beans, and to compensate for the loss of the clover more vetches are planted in the root quarter.

I do not think there is any extended acreage of root or green crops grown except the vetches before mentioned after which we get some very good turnips, but a greater bulk is grown now where there is a liberal use of artificials than was formerly the case with farmyard manure and less artificial.

As I said we are on the Cotswold hills, you may imagine the Cotswold sheep are kept here, which they were a few years ago almost to a farm, but, since the advance in the price of the black-faced mutton, the Oxford Down is taking the place of the heavier white-faced sheep on many farms. The cattle usually kept are shorthorns.

The sheep are now kept almost entirely within the hurdles whereas they formerly ran loose in the fields during the summer months. I remember when I was a boy we used to pack the hurdles in a shed about the beginning of May and there they remained until October but now we never think of having a hurdle in the dry. There is certainly more mutton produced. I usually fed out 300 sheep during the year on 480 acres, but I suppose this would be above the average, I should think about half a sheep to the acre would be about the quantity of mutton produced in this district. There is very little beef or pork produced.

I should compute the increase in corn produced per

acre to be 4 bushels per acre more than it was twenty years ago but still I should be afraid to say there was much more corn produced in the district now than formerly, as, since the rise in wages took place, several farmers have allowed their land to remain down to seeds longer and have turned their attention to the production of more mutton.

I should imagine the employment of artificial manures, feeding stuffs etc have increased by one third within the last twenty years.

The steam cultivator is used considerably as an auxiliary, as in consequence of the corn and hay-cutting being done with the horses the work is apt to get behind. The double-furrow horse ploughs are used to a certain extent but I am no advocate for them as I find I can do my ploughing better and cheaper with a pair of horses on to a single two-wheel plough.

The reaper and mower are generally used. The economical results following the use of the reaping and mowing machines are considerable, as, for instance, while the grass is being cut with the mower the men are invaluable cutting out the swedes. The corn is cut and tied at little more than half the expense with the aid of the reaper.

Wages have increased about 25 per cent. With regard to rent on many estates it has risen five and in some places ten per cent, while on others it remains the same as twenty years ago.

Of other burdens it is difficult to speak with any like

exactness as there are few farms that are affected in the same way from the same local causes, as for instance where there has been a school board formed and new schools erected, it has fallen very heavy on the land and some parishes have a large amount of turnpike roads fallen on them which increases the burdens considerably.

This retrospect serves to confirm Thomas West Porter's patient submission to the hand of God. Only the reference to trends in rent hint at the traumatic impact of the Great Agricultural Depression. In 1902 Thomas wrote a poem, entitled *Thine, Ever Thine*, later used as a Brethren hymn. It shows his belief in a 'daily walk with God'. The following are the first and last verses:

> O Lord, how blest – as day by day
> We pass along our pilgrim way –
> To know that we are Thine.
> Thine – by redemption's precious blood
> Which saved, which brought us nigh to God
> In righteousness divine.
>
> Then may we always own Thy claim,
> And overcoming in Thy name,
> From earthliness be free,
> And by the hidden manna fed,
> Renewed in strength, the path we'd tread
> Which leads us up to Thee.

Chapter Nine
FAMILY, CHURCH AND BRETHREN

homas West Porter was twenty-seven years old when he married Mary Jane Waine of Great Barrington in the parish church on 25 October 1871. In the parish register Thomas was described as a bachelor farmer of Holwell, Oxfordshire, son of Humphrey Porter, farmer, and Mary Jane as aged twenty-eight, spinster daughter of Richard Waine, farmer, deceased. The witnesses were Thomas's older brother, John Wise Porter, Mary Jane's younger brother Richard Henry, and her sisters, Sarah Anne and Susannah.

The poem which Thomas West Porter's mother Mary wrote to celebrate their marriage suggests that theirs was a longstanding relationship – farming couples traditionally waited to marry until they had the means to set up on their own account.

> Go happy youth, at length the day is come
> That thou shalt claim thine own, the much lov'd one;
> Oh! may that love be never known to cease,
> But ever, ever, with thy years increase.
> She leaves her mother's home to be thy Bride,
> Then may she always in thy love confide;

Passing through life, so as that love to claim,

And e'en to death thy confidence retain.

Oh! May God bless you both, and may you shew

Your love to Him while sojourning below,

By ever helping such as are distressed

And, rest assured, your efforts will be blest.

Gerald, the first of Thomas and Mary Jane's seven children, was born in January 1873. His father's account books record the purchase of a crib for £1 16s and, a few months later, a perambulator for £1 15s. Dr Cheatle, the Burford practioner, attended Mary Jane during her confinements; he had the assistance of Mrs Hopes. Gerald's sister Evelyn Mary was born in 1875 and brother Garnet West two years later.

Thomas West Porter with Mary Jane, Gerald and Evelyn, c. 1877.

Thomas West Porter with Garnet, c. 1883.

Always a sickly boy Garnet, died when he was sixteen. In June 1878 Edith Susannah was born, a Down's Syndrome baby. Thomas West Porter first mentioned her condition when she was eighteen months old. On 'the last night of the year 1880' he wrote 'Dear little Edith is a cause of anxiety, how far she may be wanting in reason as she grows up we cannot see, but of this I am assured that the ways of the Lord are good and that He has a wise design in all things and will help us to bear our cross'. On the 'tenth anniversary of our marriage day', 25 October 1881, he returned to the subject. Edith's 'mental deficiency' was 'a needs-be trial'. In the census of 1891 Edith was categorised as 'imbecile'.

Caring for four small children, two of them frail, coupled with the demanding role of a farmer's wife, seems to have sapped Mary Jane's health and energy. Gerald, her eldest child, describes her baking bread and wrestling with the gander. Graham, her fifth, had no such memories, as he was not yet four years old when she died. The census enumerator who listed the household at Manor Farm in April 1881, noted the presence of a governess and a housemaid.

At this time, towards the end of Mary Jane's fifth pregnancy, her husband was wracked with anxiety. The previous summer Mary Jane had been very ill, 'brought down to the very borders of the grave'. The entry in Thomas's diary for 14 August 1881 is a plea to God to spare his dear wife 'in her coming trial, in all her pains and weakness . . . My neighbour Mr B is expecting daily to lose his partner by a most painful disorder and to be left with a large family without a mother's care. What a trial. How could I bear it? O Lord spare me.'

Four days later, on Thursday 18 August, his mood was very different. 'How little I thought when I wrote down a few of my feelings and anxious cares last Sunday evening that I should so soon have been able to raise the song of thanksgiving to my heavenly Father for He hath given my dear wife a safe confinement and hath given us another son . . . We desire to consecrate him to Thee'. This son was Graham Lane Porter. Eliza Anne, known as Lizzie, was born two years later;

Kathleen Jane, born in 1885, completed the family.

Thomas West Porter's account books describe a household which combined many of the characteristics of the traditional farm, which Gerald portrayed in his memoirs, and those of a middle-class late Victorian house: payments for 'use of boar' and the hops and malt to brew Manor Farm beer sit alongside bills for life assurance, a hat stand, picture frames, piano tuning and flowers and rose trees for the garden.

Thomas West Porter was a gospel Christian brought up in a devout household: he was particularly close to his mother Mary. A letter he sent her on 8 September 1881, shortly before her death, illustrates the nature of the faith learned at her knee and the spiritual anguish he experienced in the early 1880s.

> I very much hoped to have heard that you were a good deal better than when I saw you but I am afraid from the tone of your letter that you have not improved much. I cherish the hope still that it may be God's will that you may yet regain your normal health and strength, but I know that He can, in His own gracious and loving way, compensate even for the loss of health by revealing Himself more clearly and sweetly to our souls. I trust that He has done so with you and that you have been enabled very much to enjoy the assurance of His forgiving mercy in Jesus Christ, and it is my earnest prayer that, if you are for a time prevented from attending the House of Prayer, our God and Father may make it known to your soul that He dwelleth not only in Temples made with hands and that He can make those that tarry at home divide the spoil.

I should very much like to have heard Mr Wilmot on the text you mentioned 'Who indeed but our God that sends the showers?' But, oh, this rebellious, unbelieving heart of mine, is slow to trace the hand of a loving Father in the dispensations of His providence and so ready to set up my own will in opposition to His. Mr Goddard[50] preached from that text on the 6th of March, 'Be of good cheer. It is I, be not afraid.' And I thank God there was one to whom he was permitted to minister comfort. I think I said when writing to you before what a comfort it is to know that our salvation depends not upon our changeable frames and feelings but upon the convenanted mercies of our unchanging God in Christ, who has said, 'I have loved thee with an everlasting love'.

The more one sees of one's sinful heart and the depths of sin to which, but for God's grace, we should at any moment fall, the more comfort is derived from this blessed truth.

I have for some time past been in the habit of noting down any thought the Lord in His mercy may be pleased to give me on any portion of His word or on any special act of providence and a few days since the following was written. It was, however, not intended for any eye but my own, so please keep it as such. But, as I was writing to you, it occurred to me that the thoughts therein expressed may be comforting to yourself as they have been to me, if so, they will not have been written in vain.

---

[50] The parson who served Holwell.

September 5th. This morning I read a part of the 3rd chapter of Joshua and again this evening it was the portion chosen for our family reading for the subject has been in my heart all day and tonight I would humbly thank my God, the Holy Spirit, for that He hath fed me with this sweet morsel . . . – Here then I find Joshua and the children of Israel coming to Jordan and lodging there before passing over. Now, my soul, remember thou hast a Jordan of death to pass over and will it not be profitable for thee to be . . . lodging near there in contemplation . . . lest the summons come upon thee unawares? Dost thou not see here a type of thy Saviour Jesus Christ and has He not passed this river before thee?

Yet, blessed be God, He has, and has parted the waters assunder, and has dispelled the darkness of the valleys of death and opened the gate of heaven to all believers . . .

> And, oh, when I have safely passed
> Through every conflict but the last,
> Unchanging still, he'll stand beside
> My dying bed, for he has died,
> Then point to realms of endless day
> And wipe the latest tear away.

Your affectionate Son
TWP

At Holwell, he served as churchwarden and taught in the Sunday school. His household at Manor Farm was saturated with the words of scripture. As we have seen he took to heart the almanac's thought for the day. (Nineteenth-century almanacs fell into two broad categories: those which claimed to foretell the future and those which provided a compendium of useful information 'uncontaminated by astrology or prediction'.) Incidents in his children's young lives were parables. In January 1884 Thomas wrote:

> What lessons my dear Lord often teaches me by my own litle ones . . . The one today has shown the quietness and satisfaction that follows the consciousness of being guided by the Father's hand. It was in this way: As my little boy was running about the yards with me he kept continuously asking me the question, 'Where are we going now, Father?' As soon as I had answered the little questioner and we had visited the place, he immediately asked again – 'And where are we going now, Father?' But presently he came and put his hand in mine and then, I noticed, the questions ceased. There was evidently the sense that he was going where his Father led him and that was enough . . .
>
> The other lesson was that of restoration. Another of my little ones about three years old[51] was a naughty boy at breakfast time and, after repeatedly correcting him, I was obliged to say that, unless he ceased his naughtiness, I must take him from the table up into the nursery and, as the wayward spirit continued, I was obliged, both for my word's sake and his good to do as I said. He cried and sobbed bitterly and I left him so and went about my

---

[51] Graham Lane Porter.

morning work and forgot for the time the little incident. But when I came in some hours afterwards, he was just being brought in from a walk and no sooner did he get his hat off than he ran to me and put up his face to be kissed nor would he be satisfied until he had received one and kissed me in return. Now, I thought, what a beautiful picture of the believer's restoration after falling into sin. My little teacher had incurred my displeasure and called forth my chastisement but did he cease to be my son? Of course he did not.

In front of Manor Farm, c. 1887. Seated in pony trap left to right: Graham, Lizzie, Edie, Kathleen, with their father Thomas West Porter. The housekeeper Mrs Williams is standing at the front door.

189

Yet, between October 1878 and the spring of 1884, Thomas West Porter laboured under an overwhelming sense of sin and an unassuagable spiritual thirst. He considered the agricultural depression 'a judgment for our sins, nationally and individually'. Though their marriage was happy, he and Mary Jane had 'a cross to bear in the mental deficiency' of their daughter Edith. That mark of the hand of God 'we know full well, but how much worse do we deserve?' A succession of sudden deaths troubled him. He commented on an acquaintance, who, 'at midday was in apparently good health and spirits and in the evening was a corpse'. His sister Susannah died 'her mouth and tongue swollen as to make her unrecognizable'. Death also came to

> . . . the wife of our friend and relative J. Holton . . . just settled as they were in their new home . . . I ask why did the blow fall on my friend and not on myself? The circumstances of our cases were very similar, both his children and our own were stricken with measles, his wife took it, which brought on a premature confinement and in a few short hours ended in death . . .

In April 1883 he noted:

> Within the last few days our God has again been teaching us lessons of our own mortality. First by taking away a mother from three little ones. Her clothes caught fire and before it could be put out, she had such injuries that, after a little more than a week of intense suffering, she died . . . And then again there is one in this village who has

been called to pass through great bodily pain and is now evidently very near his end.

Although he was on excellent terms with Daniel Goddard, the parson, an Oxford graduate by this time in his seventies, Thomas West Porter found little comfort in his church.

Thomas had first come into contact with the Brethren in 1870 when he met Mrs Pinnell, the wife of his predecessor at Manor Farm. She had asked him to attend a meeting held in one of the barns at Holwell. According to his son Gerald, the preacher on that occasion was Mr J. S. Oliphant. In later years Thomas was very much influenced by Thomas Henry Reynolds of Burford, a leading member of the Brethren.

In the weeks before Christmas 1881 Thomas 'made the acquaintance of Mr Champney of Cambridge' – Henry D'Arcy Champney was a member of Corpus, who graduated and was ordained in 1878. For the next four years Champney served St Andrew the Less in the town; but in 1883 he disappeared from the official listing of Anglican clergy – Crockfords's Clerical Directory. With Champney Thomas West Porter

> . . . enjoyed Christian fellowship. He was an ordained clergyman in the Church of England with great abilities to preach and a large field of labour opened up to him in Cambridge but yet he was so led by the Holy Spirit to see that he was not where God wanted him to be that he was enabled to come out and join [the] Brethren.

He began to 'read some of the works' and attend 'a good many of the meetings of the Brethren at Burford'. He felt 'very much drawn towards them'. In December 1883, on a convalescent holiday in Eastbourne, Thomas West Porter providentially

> . . . met with Mr Oliphant through his almost losing his train. For, although holding a second class ticket, yet he was obliged to rush into a third class compartment where I was sitting in order to catch the train at all . . . Just as we reached the place where we were to part, I discovered that he was the person whom I heard preach in a barn at Holwell twelve years ago. O that men would praise the Lord for His good and declare the wonders that He doeth to the children of men.

On 23 March 1884, 'in reading the fourteenth chapter of Exodus', Thomas West Porter was convinced that the commandment God gave to the Israelites as they went out of Egypt – 'Go forth' – was meant for him:

> I asked Mr G[52] to release me from the duties[53] which I could no longer conscientiously fulfil. He raised no objection . . . Also to release me from the office of Churchwarden . . . so, thank God, I am free from that which has far too long held me in bondage.

He was jubilant: 'My soul is now like a bird escaped from the snare of the fowler. The snare is broken. I am delivered. '

---

[52] The parson.

[53] In the Sunday School.

Membership of the Exclusive Brethren was an appropriate terminus for Thomas West Porter's spiritual pilgrimage. They were a nineteenth century manifestation of a recurrent tendency in the Christian tradition: the rejection of institutions and ceremonies without scriptural precedent. They rejected an ordained clergy in favour of a ministry of believers. They celebrated the Lord's Supper, breaking bread and taking wine, using the humblest of everyday utensils. Theirs was a community of theologians, reading and interpreting the scriptures. Conversational Bible study was their means of sharing and affirming their belief. A community of believers, they avoided contact with other Christians and those whom they perceived as indifferent. Brethren met not in churches but in whatever indoor space was offered to them: a stable loft, a clock factory. At Manor Farm it was the wash house. In March 1884, Thomas West Porter wrote:

> I would also mention a little incident connected with the opening of this place [the wash house] for prayer and preaching. When it became too cold to have an open air service any longer, we were led to look round to see if a place could be found suitable to meet in during the winter months. The wash house was the only place that presented itself and myself and two fellow Christians went in one night after an open-air meeting and it was suggested to lay the matter at once before the Lord and ask His guidance and direction so we repaired to the throne of grace upon the subject and while so engaged, the servant girl, not knowing we were there, locked the door. And, as the place was detached, to be locked in meant being there for the night or at least giving us some

trouble to liberate ourselves. We however, made ourselves heard before she turned away from the door.

His son Gerald remembered the meetings:

> On Sundays Gospel preachings were held in this wash house for many years, with interest and blessing I think. The forms were stacked overhead and got down and arranged on Saturday, this being a duty assigned to the houseman, Mark Pratley. A roaring fire was kindled in the cold weather, in front of which the preacher stood, so very frequently he waxed warm, and on one ocasion too much so and had to resort to one of the coppers as a pulpit.

In later years the kitchen was used for these meetings, which Shepherd Winfield, among others, attended. He always sat in a Windsor armchair, still in the family and still known as 'Shepherd's chair'. Bob, the family dog, lived in the kitchen but, at the mention of the word 'books' – hymn books and bibles – he would get up and go out.

In April 1884, only a week after Thomas had left the Church of England, 'dear Mr Goddard' the Holwell parson, 'being in his usual health . . . was making his way home from Bradwell Grove when he was taken ill on the road'. By the time his manservant had summoned help, 'he was gone': another intimation that 'we are dying mortals'; and, for Thomas West Porter, confirmation that God had willed his decision to leave the Anglican Church:

> But Oh! how manifest is the Lord's hand in leading me about. It makes me feel lost in wonder when I consider

how that there had long been a resolution that at Mr Goddard's removal I should certainly cease to be in any way connected with the Church of England.

Just over a year later, on 15 May 1885, Mary Jane died.

. . . for nearly fourteen years [she was] my loved companion, truly she was the sharer of my joys and sorrows. I can only cherish her memory with deepest affection, but now she is gone not lost but gone before. The Lord had need of her.

Thomas West Porter wrote a full and moving account of her last days:

It was rather more than three weeks since she had given birth to our seventh child[54] and all had seemed to go on well, when she took a severe chill which settled on her lungs and was the cause, 'humanly speaking', of her death. As I returned home one Saturday evening after a few hours' absence, I found she had already gone to bed, and I saw, from her flushed cheek and shortness of breath, that something serious was the matter, but hoped that a good night's sleep would restore, or at least alleviate, the suffering. This, however, she did not obtain but passed the night restless and in pain, with scarcely any sleep.

In the morning, the Doctor was sent for and applied remedies which we still hoped would effect a cure, but

---

[54] Kathleen.

the Lord in his sovereign wisdom ordered it otherwise . . .

But now another trial came upon us, our second boy[55], eight years old, had been ailing for some days and his illness began to take such a serious form that for some days we thought he was going to be taken from us, this was a time of terrible exercise and earnest pleading with the Lord in his behalf. He however gave us comfort by His words, 'Believe on the Lord Jesus Christ and thou shalt be saved <u>and thy house</u>. Acts XVI 31'. We can now thank Him that He has taken away the sickness and restored him to health, and Oh! may the life which He has thus preserved be devoted to Himself and to His glory. Towards the Tuesday week after my dear Wife was taken ill he began to shew signs of improvement which enabled me to turn my attention more entirely to her who until now (the Doctor said) had been holding her own but whose illness began to assume alarming symptoms. Hour after hour we watched and hoped for some sign of improvement, but still it came not, she patiently suffered on, ever thankful for any little attention shewn to her. The Tuesday and Wednesday nights were passed with scarcely any sleep and that little was disturbed and unrefreshing. She thoroughly realized how very ill she was . . . On Thursday morning she was not so well. The Doctor came three times during the day to see her, and at night he told me that her state was extremely critical and she was losing strength. When he was gone, she asked

---

[55] Garnet.

me what he said and I replied that he said she was getting weaker. I saw a shade of sadness pass over her face for a moment . . . then she turned to me (and with a look of resignation; which never again left her) she said, 'Dearest, I had hoped that the Lord would have been pleased to raise me up again but I see it is not His will. I know it will be a great trial to you for me to leave you but my Saviour will sustain you and I can trust you in His hands and all the dear children, every one. He will take care of you all'.

She now cast off all reserve and began to talk (as freely as the shortness of her breath would allow) to each one as they came to her bedside of the unsearchable riches of Christ her Saviour, who she lost no opportunity of magnifying and she begged all to come to Him that they might meet her again, where she said, there will be no more pain, no more sorrow, and no more parting and she spoke with the earnestness of one who felt the importance of what she spoke . . . It was painful to witness the amount of physical labour she had to employ to obtain breath . . . Her face continued to wear such a peaceful, happy expression that it was hard to realize that it was a bed of death. She several times quoted the first two verses of the twenty-seventh Psalm. [The Lord is my light and my salvation: whom shall I fear? The Lord is the strength of my life: of whom shall I be afraid? When the wicked, even mine enemies and my foes, came upon me to eat up my flesh, they stumbled and fell.]

Once when I could not keep back my tears, I said I

197

reproached myself for my sorrow when I saw her so happy.

She said, 'I am happy and it is all through Jesus and his precious blood. A poor wretched sinner like me could do nothing to prepare myself for death and the presence of the Lord, but He has done it all'.

I said, 'Thanks be to God' and she took the words out of my lips and added 'Which giveth us the victory through our Lord Jesus Christ'.

And then she said, 'O death, where is thy sting. O grave, where is thy victory?'

Thursday night was passed without sleep, and the shortness of breath with a trying cough and the difficulty of expectoration continued. Still, however, she took nourishment in the form of Beef Tea etc. Friday morning arrived with no better symptoms and, as we looked to the previous day, we could not hide from ourselves the fact that she was now much weaker. We knew that the Lord was taking her and that she was soon to know the joy of being with Him who loved her. Yet how slow poor nature was to give her up, looking even until now for some sign of improvement.

I looked for the text on the almanac and told her that it was this, 'The Lord is nigh unto them that are of a broken heart, Psalm XXXIV. 18'.

. . . Her mind now began to wander a good deal but she was still able to collect herself when we spoke to her . . . We also once more read a few verses from her favourite Psalm. She said to me about midday, 'The

Doctor thought I should scarcely last through the night and I am still here, what is the Lord leaving me for?' I said, 'You are waiting to depart and go with Christ, which is far better.' 'Yes', she said 'which is far better', laying great emphasis on the word.

In the afternoon she constantly wandered, so that several times we doubted if she would ever gain consciousness again. Her brother came to see her about this time and, after he had spoken to her and had taken a seat, she lay and looked earnestly at him for some time without speaking, and I was questioning in my mind whether she would be able to do so when she called him to her and said: 'I am soon going but I can leave all with perfect resignation in the hands of Him who has done so much for me. He will take care of all. He has saved me by His precious blood. 'Tis all through him that I am able to lie here with peace and joy, if it were not, I could not do so but should be tossing about giving everybody a lot of trouble. I trust you will believe on Him too and meet me up there.'

I said to her afterwards, 'I see that the Lord has been leaving you here to preach the gospel to us yet'. She said, 'I am waiting and He will soon be here.'

It was about four o'clock and, as we sat watching her, she became rather restless for a little while, raising herself on her elbow and arranging her pillow. I asked her if she would not like to see our two eldest children and she intimated that she would. And I then left the room to fetch them and was gone only a few minutes.

When I returned, I just heard her say, 'This is the joy of a mother's heart.' I then took the children to her to give her the last kiss. But she failed to recognise or to speak to them, and lay with fixed eyes and gradually shortening breath for a few minutes, when, without a struggle she breathed her last and her spirit departed to be with Him who had loved her and given Himself for her. Who can imagine what that moment was to her? To us it was one of the deepest sorrow for our loss, yet mingled with a sanctified joy because of her eternal gain . . .'

Thomas West Porter labelled the manuscript from which these extracts come: 'Sustaining grace in the hour of death, as manifested in the departure of M-J-P'. The only memento which he kept of his dear Mary Jane was a note, still in its little envelope. There is no date but perhaps it was written in 1877 as the accounts for that year record £1 7s 6d spent on repairs to a trap.

Dear Tom

No doubt William will tell you what an accident he had – drove into Mrs Garlick's perambulator and empty bottles. You may fancy I was frightened. It was just by Mr Bides. I think Polly turned a little towards the Farm, Mrs G. did not turn out quite so far as she should have done and I fancy Wm. was nodding so over went the perambulator and luckily empty bottles out onto the street. Broke one bottle. She directly claimed £1 0s 0d damages. I told her I would see her presently. I have been up, she is very sorry she said so much, did not know me but I went to Wheeler, he was not at home so

Jessie has fetched it down. It was one wheel broken but Jessie says he can make it stronger than before by three o'clock so I can soon put it all straight with her. Poor old Billy is so vexed. Hope you will get on all right. Take care of yourself. They are all well.

With Fondest love

Believe me ever your affec wife

Mary J. Porter

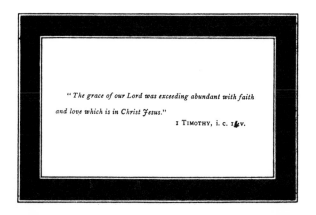

Mary Jane's memorial card.

Mary Jane Porter's death left an understated, poignant mark in her husband's accounts: between the items '[horse] collar maker, £5 3s 10d' and 'lamb dipper, £1 0s 1d' there is 'funeral & mourning exps, etc, £11 8s 6d'.

Thomas West Porter had need for 'sustaining grace'. The last entry in his spiritual notebooks suggests that, in the throes of bereavement, he had to cope with the secular consequences of his rejection of the Church of England. He wished to be faithful to God but also 'respectful to those to whom honour is due'. However, as he observed:

> It is clear that I have incurred the displeasure of those in high estate by separating myself from their company and commands.

His name is not mentioned but the clear implication is that Thomas West Porter had fallen foul of his landlord William Henry Fox.

> The Lord has been pleased lately to bring many into the little meetings here to hear the Gospel, may it be something more than mere curiosity.

To 'Squire' Fox, patron of the parish church, who noted absentees and looked for explanations for their absence, the services in the wash house at Manor Farm were both a spiritual and political affront. The tenancy of Manor Farm, like the hirings of farm servants, ran from Michaelmas to Michaelmas with the promise, but not the security of renewal. The final words of the notebook are:

> Yea O Lord our God, Thou canst Make even the wrath of man turn to Thy praise, may it be so now, I would humbly beseech Thee, for Jesus Christ's sake.

The breach with the 'Squire' was not permanent. Graham Lane Porter could remember going to the party given at Bradwell Grove to celebrate Queen Victoria's Golden Jubilee in 1887. (Eighty years later he assured his family that when the old Queen's body was brought back from Osborne in 1901 the gun salute which boomed out over the Solent could be heard in Oxfordshire. Of course, the countryside was quieter then: the loudest man-made noises came from the steam engines on the railways and on the land.)

It was almost inevitable that Thomas West Porter would remarry. His mother and his mother-in-law were both dead, so were his sisters, Susannah and Elizabeth; Mary Craddock was a busy farmer's wife. 'A large family' needed 'a mother's care'. For a member of the Brethren, who shunned marriage with outsiders, his choice was restricted. Ann Lunn, whom he took as his second wife in November 1887, less than two and a half years after Mary Jane's death, was the daughter of a neighbouring farmer. She was a woman of his own age, in her forties, and lived in the London suburb of Sidcup. Because the Brethren had no meeting places licensed for marriages, the wedding took place at the Register Office at Bromley. Thomas West Porter and his new wife spent their honeymoon in the Isle of Wight.

In preparation for Ann's arrival at Manor Farm, Thomas had spent over £15 on a new coal-fired 'Kitchener' stove. He also purchased a carriage from Mary Jane's Uncle William Lane of Broadfield. It was old and in need of repairs – the repairs cost almost twice as much as the purchase price of £6. Ann had some of the rooms redecorated soon after she moved in. The family remembered her as 'plain by name, looks and nature'. In his old age Graham Lane Porter recalled her as a hard woman who showed great favouritism to his sister Kathleen. One memory seemed to sum up her nature: she bought Graham a pair of boots which were too small for him. All the same, she made him wear them, scolding him as an ungrateful and complaining child. His feet were deformed as a result; he suffered from hammer toes for the rest of his life.

Gerald, Evelyn and Garnet went to private schools. (The boys were pupils of Mr Champney in Cambridge, the man whose influence had been an important factor in persuading their father to leave the Church of England.) Graham started his education at the village school 'a matter of two or three hundred yards, sometimes being hurried by the sissle and open beaks of the geese following me. I took with me 1d or it might be 2d every Monday morning to pay for the education I received'.

Since farmers, and other employers, had strong reservations about sending their children to school with their workers, it may be that Graham's attendance at the village school was a consequence of the hard times farmers were going through in the 1880s.

In 1891, when he was ten, Graham left the village school for Burford Grammar School. He walked the three miles there and back. Then, to his long-lasting regret, after only two terms, he was sent as a boarder to Mr Thursfield's tiny Brethren school at Witney where he had a very restricted education. He started work on his father's farm the Christmas before his sixteenth birthday.

Garnet West Porter, considered too frail for a farming life, had been apprenticed to a draper, a member of the Brethren, at Hemel Hempstead. H. G. Wells, the son of a Bromley shopkeeper, described his unhappy experience as a draper's apprentice at Messrs Rodgers and Denyer's establishment in Windsor in his *Experiment in Autobiography*. His indentures were signed in 1880.

I was taken up the narrow staircase to the men's dormitory, in which were eight or ten beds and four miserable wash handbasins and I was shown a dismal little sitting-room with a ground glass window opening on to a blank wall in which the apprentices and assistants might 'sit' of an evening, and then I was conducted downstairs to an underground dining room, lit by naked gas-jets and furnished with two long tables covered in American cloth, where the eating was to be done. Then I was introduced to the shop and, particularly, to the cash desk, where it had been arranged for the first year of my apprenticeship that I was to sit on a tall stool and receive money, give change, enter the amount on a sheet and stamp receipts . . .

I was to come down at half past seven in the morning . . . without fail, dust, clean windows, eat a bread-and-butter breakfast at half past eight, prepare my cash sheet and so to the routine of the day. I had to add up my cash at the end of the day, count the money in the till, make sheet and cash agree, help to wrapper-up and sweep out the shop, and so escape at half past seven or eight to drink the delights of freedom until ten, when I had to be in. Lights out at half past ten. And this was to go on day after day – for ever it seemed to me – with early closing day once a week at five, and Sunday free.

Garnet died of acute pneumonia at Hemel Hempstead in April 1893. His father was at his side. Thomas's mourning verses included the lines:

We feel the wrench, it makes us know
The stamp of death on all below
But while these earthly ties are riven
All is secured, through Christ in heaven.

Kathleen, her stepmother's favourite and too young to remember her natural mother, was sent to a Brethren boarding school in London. When she was taken ill in October 1897 with severe abdominal pains, the school doctor decided to operate on her on the school's kitchen table. (Although this may suggest a casual negligence, given the poor understanding of antisepsis, kitchen table surgery was the safest option for minor operations at this time.) The doctor had mistakenly diagnosed Kathleen's condition for appendicitis; she had an ovarian cyst. The death certificate recorded that she died of 'syncope shock when undergoing an operation for abdominal tumour and under influence of ether'. The inquest returned a verdict of natural causes. Kathleen was only twelve years old. She was buried alongside her mother, Mary Jane, and her brother Garnet in Holwell churchyard just a few yards from the farmhouse.

The only memento which has survived is a letter to her brothers, written six months before her death.

26 Ashley Road
Hornsey Rise
March 27th 1897

My dear Gerald and Graham

I thought you would like to have a letter from me. Last Saturday we went to Waterloo Park and Miss Ferrior was there with some of the deaf and dumb, there is a new little boy just come, he is fourteen but he looks only six is'en't sad.

Thank you very much for your letters.

Please excuse having a letter between you, it takes so long to write you one each.

Tell Mother and Evelyn their turn will come next.

We aurions[56] come home three weeks today (DV).

Mr Allen preached at Hazelville last Sunday from John III: 16 & 1 John 16.

How are all the animals now, does Bobby go out with you or is he too old, poor Bobby.

The trees are coming out now they look so pretty.

Now I must say 'Good Bye' now as I have not much to say

Please give my love to ALL.

I remain

Your loving little sister

Kathleen

Her father recorded his reflections on her death in his verses 'On the death of a child, 12 years, who fell asleep after a short illness'.

The Shepherd of the flock surveys the whole
With careful gaze when He's about to cull,
A lamb may be the object of His choice,
He calls, the lambkin answers to His voice.

---

[56] She was showing off her French.

207

In front of the summer house in the garden of Manor Farm, c. 1895.

Standing left to right: Graham, Evelyn, Gerald, Lizzie. Seated left to right: Kathleen, Thomas West, Ann, Edith (Edie), with Bobby the dog in front.

In this verse Thomas West Porter was writing directly from his experience: sheep kept as he kept his, penned and used to looking to their shepherd for their food, recognize and respond to a particular voice:

> . . . The hearts of Friends may grieve and tears may flow
> Feeling the break up of things here below,
> But while their bosoms with emotions swell
> Faith looks above, assured that all is well.

Membership of the Brethren shaped the family's responses to bereavement – and their daily lives. They kept Sunday strictly as the Lord's Day. No games or toys were allowed except for the Noah's Ark which had been made by 'one of the labourers', according to Lizzie.

Noah's Ark – the only toy allowed on Sundays.

209

The children were also allowed to look at photographs of views of the Holy Land through a stereoscope which, as its name suggests, produced an impression of a three-dimensional image. Even when they were young adults Thomas West Porter would not permit his sons to ride their bicycles on Sunday. However, one hot Sunday, after they had worked late into the previous evening in the hayfield, Graham recalled, he was allowed to ride to Burford to the Meeting, rather than walk the two miles. They always cycled after that. Thomas's Down's Syndrome daughter Edith, little Edie, as she was known in the family, went to the Meeting and learned the names of Jacob's twelve sons by heart. When she repeated the list, she added 'Shepherd's dog' when she got to Dan, and 'Bodman' after Benjamin.

The deaths of Garnet and Kathleen were not the only signals of 'the breaking up of things at Manor Farm'. The surviving children were coming of age. In 1901 Evelyn, the eldest of Thomas West Porter's daughters, married Harold Hindley, who owned an iron foundry in Bourton in Dorset; he helped to set up William Richard Morris's first car factory at Cowley, now on the outskirts of Oxford. Their children remembered Morris as the man who smoked a cigar in their house, something utterly forbidden in a Brethren household. Gerald began to farm on his own account. Edie and Lizzie her younger sister, who cared for her until Edie died at the age of fifty-eight, continued to live at home and moved with their father and stepmother to Burford when their brother Graham took over the tenancy of Manor Farm in 1910.

Part Four

GLOUCESTERSHIRE

Chapter Ten

THE PORTERS
AND THE WESTS

y comparison with their successors, the lives of Thomas West Porter's father Humphrey (1798-1889) and his grandfather John Porter (1757-1851) are poorly documented. Neither left accounts. John's will, if indeed he made one, has not survived. The richest sources derive from two members of the West family: Humphrey's wife Mary and her brother Thomas, whose papers descended to his great-nephew Graham Lane Porter.

John Porter, Thomas's grandfather, married Mary Dunford, of Great Barrington, on 23 June 1788, and the baptisms of the first five of their six children are recorded in the registers of that parish. They were Richard, Ann, Mary, Humphrey and John, who were born between 1789 and 1800, and lastly Benjamin who was baptised at Little Barrington in 1804. Theirs was a long-lived and close-knit generation.

John was ninety-three when he died in 1851, though the census of that year states his age as ninety-five. He was living in Great Barrington with his daughters Mary, aged fifty-six, and Jane aged fifty-four. Jane is something of a mystery; her given age argues against the suggestion thst she might be identified with Anne, who was baptised in

1792. His granddaughter Helen Mary, who was seven, was also staying in the house on 30 March, the night of the census. After a long life that spanned the reigns of five monarchs, John was buried in the churchyard at Little Barrington.

John had lived through stirring times abroad and at home. He was a young man at the outbreak of the American War of Independence; in his maturity during the quarter century defined by the French Revolution and the Napoleonic Wars but, almost without doubt, the drama which touched his life most closely was the epidemic of violence which raged in the English countryside between 1830 and 1831: historians have plotted no fewer than 1500 separate incidents. Studies of the outburst point to a constellation of contributory factors. Some farmers who had done well out of the wars against France had adopted a gentrified way of life which set them apart from their men. Peace was accompanied by a drop in their incomes but the wages they paid their workers fell more sharply. In arable districts, seasonal unemployment was common. The price of bread, the staple diet of the poor, remained high. In consequence, many labouring families were reduced to dependence on the poor rates collected from their better-off neighbours. The spread of horse-powered threshing tackle seemed certain to exacerbate their difficulties – 390 were destroyed in the fifteen months of unrest. The pattern of disturbances reflected the misery of the labourers in the corn-growing counties – rioting, arson and machine-breaking were concentrated in the south of the country and East Anglia.

On 26 November 1830 violence erupted in the Eastern Cotswolds. Thrashing tackle was destroyed at Eastleach Turville on the 28th. At Southrop on the 29th 'a great mob' assembled, 'many of them armed with hammers, axes and bludgeons'. Outsiders may have sparked off the Southrop riot, a farmer from Langford in Oxfordshire testified that two of the ringleaders had taken part in a disturbance at Langford earlier in the day. According to George Swinford, who wrote the *History of Filkins*, 'At Southrop the owner of the manor appeared to give [the rioters] a welcome and ordered beer all round'. His action was not unprecedented. Landowners and farmers elsewhere made conciliatory responses to mobs which confronted them. On 28 October Sir John Filmer had given money 'for refreshments' to the crowd which assembled outside East Sutton Park, his house near Maidstone. Some farmers stood by while their thrashing tackle was smashed, others positively encouraged their destruction. A significant proportion of the machines were insured or owned by syndicates and, even where an individual farmer faced the prospect of bearing the cost alone, it was less daunting than the threat of fire. At Southrop, according to Swinford, many of the rioters were disabled by drink; 'the County Yeomanry soon arrived and arrested the ringleaders'.

Of the 94 Gloucestershire men tried at the Quarter Sessions, 41 were acquitted, 26 gaoled and 27 transported to Van Diemen's Land, as Tasmania was then known. The Directors of the Van Diemen's Land Company, who included Joseph Cripps MP, a local landowner and Chairman of the County Quarter Sessions, did their best to recruit the transportees as workers for their own holdings on the island. As they argued, 'with the exception of the crime for which they were expatriated', these men 'were considered free from crime . . . an opportunity for securing such labourers will never again occur'. Their scheme to improve the quality of their labour force at a stroke was frustrated by the Colonial Office.

Although the term of transportation was fixed at seven or fourteen years, none of the men returned. Fragments of evidence suggest that some of the Gloucestershire men did quite well for themselves in Van Diemen's Land – very few of those who were acquitted at the Quarter Sessions ended their lives as farmers, shopkeepers, publicans or independent craftsmen. However, the plight of women and children left behind in England was wretched. Mrs Sturge Gretton remembered a woman from Burford, just over the county boundary in Oxfordshire, who died sixty years later 'in her chair turned towards the east because she had heard that it was out of the sunrise travellers from Australia would return.'

All of John Porter's sons were farmers. The eldest and the youngest died within days of each other in 1875, aged eighty-six and seventy-one. Richard, the elder brother, had been ill for only a week and died from bronchitis; whilst the death certificate attributed Benjamin's death to 'asthenia' – general weakness. They were widowers (Benjamin for over three decades) and had shared the house at Brickpool Farm in Windrush for many years – they were together at the time of the 1851 census. Richard's daughter-in-law Jane witnessed both deaths; their shared tomb was 'erected by Helen, only child of Benjamin' and wife of William Mason, a Windrush maltster.

John Porter's daughter Mary died in 1876 at the age of eighty-two in the parish of her birth. She left her niece Helen Mason her bible and 'my small round mahogany table' – women often described their furniture with proprietorial pride in their wills. Her father's bible, embossed with his name, went to her nephew John Wise Porter (Thomas West Porter's brother). In 1994 the bible was in the custody of a third John Porter, the great-great grandson of its first owner.

Mary's younger brother John died at Fairford in 1885, as old as the century. His estate was valued at nearly £4000. Perhaps anticipating disputes over his will between his three sons and three daughters, he laid down that

> Any Child[57] who complains as to the way the goods are disposed of shall be peremptorily excluded from all benefit and it will be as if his or her name is not mentioned herein.

In 1829 John Porter's second son, Humphrey, married Mary West. Members of earlier generations of the West family lived at Wyck Rissington but Mary was born at Clapton, her mother's home parish. As a wedding present, her father gave them the bible he had received from his father-in-law 'Master Wise'. It contains notes of the births and baptisms of Mary, born in 'April 20th 1807 about half past nine o'clock in the morning and baptised May 26th 1807' and her five brothers and three sisters of whom the most important, from the point of view of Mary and her new family, was her elder brother Thomas, 'born May 15th 1799 about 2 o'clock in the morning': this bible too is still in the family. Before birth certificates were introduced in the 1830s the habit of recording children's birthdates in a family bible was widespread; before that Books of Hours, the devotional books owned by most literate people, were used to list additions to the family. The Book of Hours, now in the University Library in Cambridge, which Edmund Roberts autographed obsessively in 1553, contains a memorandum of seven births starting with 'Frank Roberts' who 'was borne the viii day of Februari anno 1570, being Shrove Sonday' and ending with 'Mary' who 'was borne 29 of June being Monday anno 1574'.

---

[57] They must have been in their fifties.

Mary Porter née West, c. 1862.

Humphrey and Mary continued the custom of recording births in another copy of the bible. (Their children were the first to be given two baptismal names.)

Mary Porter born April 24th 1831 at half past 9 o'clock in the evening at Little Barrington, Gloucestershire

Eliza Ann Porter born April 5th 1833 at 5 o'clock in the morning at Little Barrington, Gloucestershire

Susannah Porter born January 12th 1836 at 7 o'clock in the morning at Great Lemhill Farm, Oxon

Elizabeth Deborah Porter born March 21st 1838 at half past 12 o'clock in the morning at Great Lemhill Farm, Oxon

218

John Wise Porter born July 25th 1840 at half past 1 o'clock at noon at Great Lemhill Farm, Oxon

Thomas West Porter born 26th March 1844 at half past 10 o'clock in the evening at Great Lemhill Farm, Oxon and Christened at Southrop, Gloucestershire.

Great Lemhill Farm, near Southrop, 1982.

However welcome the girls were, for a farming family the eleven-year wait for a son must have been a cause of some anxiety. Humphrey and Mary ended their farming career at Great Barrington. In the 1861 census Humphrey Porter was living at Barrington Farm; the enumerator described him as a miller and farmer, aged sixty-three, with 380 acres, employing nine men and four boys and two house servants. At that time, with the exception of Susannah, all his children were still living at home.

Barrington Farm early twentieth century.

Thomas West Porter aged about eighteen, 1862.

It seems to have been from Mary Porter and her family that her children and grandchildren learned their Bible-based faith. The atmosphere she created in their household is suggested by a short, undated letter which Mary wrote towards the end of her life, indeed probably during her last illness. It begins:

> My dear Tom
>
> I was very much pleased with your letter. I have read and shed tears of joy over it many times – a verse comes so fresh to my memory as I made when you was a little boy setting on my knees, asking me questions about God and heaven . . .
>
> Be assured I do not forget you in my poor prayers and I much need yours and know you will not forget me.
>
> With fondest love, your ever affectionate, M. Porter.

At a right angle to her signature she reproduced the verse she had mentioned:

> Oh may the little prattler on my knee
> Who loves to sit and talk of God and heaven
> May he Lord Thy child by adoption be
> And know through Christ his sins to be forgiven.

Their four daughters all married farmers. Susannah, the first to marry, was twenty-two, young for a bride; her husband William Howse Smith was significantly older, indeed he seems to have discounted his age, declaring it as thirty-five; according to the census, he was sixty years old in 1871, farming 370 acres at Great Barrington with the assistance of eight men and four boys. None of Susannah's sisters married under the age of twenty-five. Mary and Eliza Ann were both thirty-one, and both married farmers from Lyneham, Oxfordshire – Mary to Robert Craddock and Eliza Ann to Robert Hewer. Elizabeth was twenty-seven and her husband a couple of years younger; he was described in the register as 'Yeoman of Kencott', a farm on the Bradwell Grove Estate where her brother Thomas West Porter was to become a tenant in the 1870s. Elizabeth died in childbirth less than a year after her marriage. Her gravestone at Great Barrington carries the following inscription:

> So teach us to number our days that we may apply our hearts to wisdom.
>
> In memory of Elizabeth Deborah the beloved wife of John Packer Wakefield (of Kencott) who departed this life June 13th 1867 aged 28 years.
>
> Behold He taketh away. Who can hinder him? Who will say unto Him what doest Thou?
>
> *Job V v 12*

Elizabeth's mother, Mary, expressed her feelings in 'Lines addressed to a Grandson on the Death of his Mother, published under the title *Breathings of a Mother's Heart.*

> My dearest boy, what shall I say to you?
> Alas, a Mother's love, who never knew;
> What shall I say? O may you meet above
> Where sorrow is unknown, where all is love.

A gentle, kind and loving Mother dear,
The few short hours that she lingered here;
Fondly she pressed her baby-boy and said,
What will become of him when I am dead?

Then calmly to her weeping friends she raised
Her dying eyes, and thus her Maker praised,
Saying, it is God's will that I should leave,
No doubt 'tis for the best, pray do not grieve.

Promise me Mother then again she said,
You will not grieve for me when I am dead;
We shall meet again in heaven I trust,
But this frail body must return to dust.

O the sad scene is ever, ever new,
When Husband, Parents, Sister, bid adieu;
Thou dear babe unconsciously didst sleep,
Knew not thy loss, then wherefore shouldst thou weep?

A fond, indulgent Husband, felt he'd lost
A doting Wife, and all his prospects crossed;
I know her memory time can ne'er erase,
Though in after years another takes her place.

A Mother too oft shed the briny tear,
For what can with a Mother's love compare?
But hush rebellious heart, nor dare complain,
Our loss we know is her eternal gain.

In spite of the anxieties which surrounded childbirth, many women had large families and made old bones: Lady Emily Lennox, mother of

223

22, died in 1814 at the age of eighty-two. (Her early start – she was fifteen when her first child was born – and her use of wetnurses to breastfeed her children explains her productivity.) But because of the risk of injury and infection, difficult births were life threatening. Most of the wives and daughters of the Porter family seem to have been fortunate in their uncomplicated labours.

Humphrey emerges from the folios of the parish registers in his old age; in the pages of the spiritual notebooks which his son Thomas kept in the 1880s and in the memory of his grandson Graham, who was eight when the old man died. Thus we see him clearly only in his eighties. On 9 February 1879 Thomas West Porter noted:

> My father told me yesterday that he was going to retire from business and I was much struck by his broken appearance . . .

Nine months later Humphrey and his wife celebrated their Golden Wedding. A card congratulating them on their long life together carries the handwritten message 'Joy and goodwishes to Mr and Mrs Porter on their Golden Wedding from Mr and Mrs Ulph. Novr 19th 1879'. In the autumn of 1881 Mary died aged seventy-five. Thomas wrote in his diary for 29 October:

> Today we have laid in her last resting place in Windrush churchyard the mortal remains of my dear mother . . . The time had come when we were compelled to hide her out of our sight. She who tenderly nursed me in my infancy, watched and prayed over me in my youth and has ever

been a most kind and indulgent Mother. Truly the memory of the just is blessed.

My dear Father is yet spared to us but, as we followed our dear mother to the grave and he walked before us leaning upon my brother's arm, bowed down with grief and with over fourscore years, we could not hide from ourselves the fact that the day of his departure cannot be far distant.

In October 1881 Humphrey had, in fact, another seven and a half years of life ahead of him. He died on 15 May 1889 at the age of ninety-one, four years to the day after his daughter-in-law Mary Jane. His grandson Graham was eight when the old man died and remembered him as a sturdy figure on horseback – a means of transport he only gave up when, at the age of ninety, he was thrown.

Humphrey Porter's will, perhaps significantly made on the fifty-second anniversary of his marriage to Mary West and a month to the day after her funeral, is striking in one respect only: its omission of any reference to his second daughter Eliza Ann, wife of Robert Hewer. Humphrey's household furniture, plate, linen, glass, china and other effects he bequeathed to his eldest son, John Wise Porter, who married a widow, Ellen Weaver, late in life. Humphrey left £100 to his eldest daughter Mary Craddock, and £100 to Raymond, only child of his fourth daughter Elizabeth Wakefield (1838-1867). A codicil, added in May 1883, stated that £100 was to be divided among the three surviving children of his third daughter Susanna Smith (1836-1882): Maria, wife of Richard Waine, Percy and Eliza. The residue of his estate, valued at £952 4s 0d, was to be divided between his sons John Wise and Thomas West Porter.

Humphrey Porter, c. 1886.

Gospel Christianity was not the only characteristic which the later generations of the Porter family learned or inherited from the Wests. Thomas West, Mary's elder brother, who farmed in Icomb, was, like his nephew and namesake Thomas West Porter, a great maker and preserver of records. His papers reflect shared concerns: farming, faith

226

and family. The business papers he left are a salutary reminder that, even in the period which later generations looked back to as a golden age, the farmer's income was unpredictable.

According to the 1851 census Thomas West and his wife Mary farmed 188 acres and employed seven men and had two live-in maids. Their twenty-two-year old daughter Mary and their twenty-year-old son Thomas were living with them.

Thomas West kept an aide-memoire of the fluctuating prices he received from cheese and wool from 1826 until his death in 1866 on a memorandum sent to him as 'Overseer of the poor of Icomb' in December 1833, reminding him 'either to send his Return of Schools . . . or explain the cause of the delay'. The figures clearly convey the message that the market for the coarse fleeces of the Cotswold sheep was shrinking and that cheesemaking was becoming unprofitable: Thomas West went over to cross-bred sheep in 1850 and reduced the size of his dairy herd from fourteen to eight.

In his usual firm hand, Thomas West transcribed onto the blue paper he habitually used, an item from the press recording the catastrophic epidemic of rinderpest which broke out in England in 1866.

The following statistical account of the Cattle Plague was copied from the Magnet Newspaper dated November 12th 1866, 'It broke out fiercely in February last, when sixteen thousand horned beasts died in a week. From that time to this 250,000 in round numbers, of animals have been attacked, 85,000 were summarily slaughtered, 125,000 died, 33,000 recovered and of 10000 no final return is made' [signed] T West

Alongside this clinical summary he preserved 'A hymn' written on white paper in an unknown and much less confident hand than his own:

> *A Hymn*
>
> *On occasion of the Cattle plague*
>
> *All creation groans and travails;*
> *Thou Oh God, shalt hear its groan;*
> *For of man and all creation*
> *Thou alike art Lord alone.*
>
> *Pity Then thy guiltless creatures,*
> *Who, not less, man's sufferings share;*
> *For our sins it is they perish;*
> *Let them profit by our prayer.*
>
> *Cast thine eye of love and mercy*

ON OCCASION OF THE CATTLE PLAGUE

All creation groans and travails;
Thou Oh God, shalt hear its groan;
For of man and all creation
Thou alike art Lord alone.

Pity then thy guileless creatures,
Who, not less, man's suffering share;
For our sins it is they perish;
Let them profit by our prayer.

Cast thine eye of love and mercy
On the misery of our Land:
Say to the destroying Angel,
'Tis enough; stay now thine hand'.

In our Homesteads, in our Valleys
Through our pasture lands give peace;
Through the Goshen of thine Israel
Bid the grievous Murrain cease.

But with deeper, tenderer pity,
Call to mind, Oh Son of God,
Those in thine own Image fashion'd;
Ransomed by thy precious blood:

Hear and grant the supplications,
Like a cloud of incense, sent
Up toward thy seat of mercy,
Through the forty days of Lent:

For the Widow, for the Orphan,
For the helpless, hopeless poor;
Helpless, hopeless, if thou spare not
Of their basket and their store.

So, while these her earnest accents
Day by day thy Church repeats,
That our Sheep may bring forth thousands
And ten thousands in our streets.

That our Oxen, strong to labour,
May not know nor fear decay;
That there be no more complaining,
And the plague have pass'd away.

And, at last to all the servants,
When earth's troubles shall be o'er,
Three-fold Godhead, give a portion
With thyself for evermore.

Amen.

In February 1866 the Cattle Disease Prevention Act was rushed through Parliament in only two weeks, with a policy of slaughter and compensation bringing the outbreak under control. By 1871 rinderpest was completely eradicated in Britain, although incidents of foot and mouth disease continued to break out from time to time.

Faith was at the core of Thomas West's life. Having concluded infant baptism had no scriptural basis, he left the Church of England and joined the Baptists, so called because they practised what they saw described in the New Testament – believers' baptism. In 1828 he applied for a licence to convert one of his barns into a Baptist chapel.

Opposite above: *'Baptist Chapel and house where the school was held':*
below: *'Interior of the Chapel'*

Two of a collection of drawings of interiors and exteriors of houses in Icomb.

To the Right Revd Father in God Folliot by Divine
permission Lord Bishop of Worcester.

We whose names are underwritten do hereby certify
that a certain Building situated in the parish of Icomb in
the county of Worcester in the possession of Thomas West
is intended to be used as a Chapel for religious worship
by Protestant Dissenters from the Church of England of
the Denomination of Baptists under and by virtue of the

Statute of the first year of King William and Queen Mary entitled 'An Act for excepting their Majesties' Protestant subjects dissenting from the Church of England from the penalty of certain laws' and also by virtue of the Statute of the fifty second year of King George the Third entitled 'An Act to repeal certain Acts relating to Religious Worship and Assemblies and persons teaching and preaching therein'.

And we request that this certificate be registered in the Commissary's Court of your Lordship.

Dated this Sixteenth day of October 1828

(signed) Thomas West

William Pratt

M West

Char Pratt

Giles Lane

5th November 1828. Registered in the Consistory Court of Worcester.

(signed) John Clifton Dy Regr.

Thomas West endorsed the document 'Certificate for holding religious worship in a Building belonging to T West at Icomb. Registered at Worcester Novr 5th 1828' and initialled it 'TW'.

Official tolerance of religious dissent was limited, and resented by some Anglicans, especially perhaps the parsons whose congregations deserted the churches for barn-chapels like the one registered at Icomb on Guy Fawkes Day 1828. When, three decades later, John Burgess, vicar of Burford, launched an attack on Baptist beliefs, Thomas West justified them in a forty-page pamphlet, *Church and Dissent,* which he published in 1865. This was not, in fact, Thomas West's first venture into print: the title page described him as 'Author of "Plain Facts in a Country Dress"'. Writing as 'A Farmer', Thomas West argued that 'a reverend divine . . . vicar of a small market town in the county of Oxford, which is seated on the river Windrush' had 'depreciate[d] and under-value[d] Dissent in an unwarrantable manner'. In the introduction he states:

> It has often been a source of grief and lamentation to us that Christians, who are the real children of God should be so frequently striving and contending with each other about religion, making a man an offender for a word, splitting hairs on some abstruse portion of God's word which, perhaps, neither party understands, making use of uncouth, harsh, and hasty expressions one towards another, and by these, and suchlike means stirring up the evil passions of fallen human nature, grieving the Holy Spirit of God, pleasing the devil, and giving the enemies of truth occasion to speak evil of them, instead of working out that golden rule given by our Lord Jesus unto His disciples, namely, 'That ye love one another' (John xiii), thus 'endeavouring to keep the unity of the spirit in the bond of peace' (Ephesians iv). But the best of men are but men at the best.'

In spite of these opening conciliatory remarks he went on to defend his strongly held beliefs, particularly repudiating infant baptism as unwarranted biblically and upholding the baptism of believers by immersion. He maintained that many of the Old Testament heroes from

234

Abel onwards were Dissenters. His closing remarks were

> We are not at all prejudiced against the Established
> Church, but we cannot receive all her teachings; neither is
> it our practice to speak evil of any denomination of
> Christians. Our motto is 'Grace be within all those that
> love our Lord Jesus Christ in sincerity' (Ephesians VI). And
> we assure the Vicar of B– that we shall be pleased to hear
> at any time that he has become a Dissenter.

Thomas West kept a copy of anonymous verses satirising the dispute.
His reaction to having gentle fun poked at so serious a subject is not
known but another, curiously incongruous, paper in his archive,
quoted later in the chapter, suggests that Thomas West may have had a
taste for mildly satirical verses:

> I've been reading your work on the Church and Dissent
> To snuff out the Vicar's Presumption you're bent,
> You are ever too kind to use words that are coarse
> And like me you will never use Physical force.
> But the Icomb extinguisher pointed and wide
> Falls flat on the Vicar's Episcopal pride.
> And out goes his light without leaving a spark,
> And Burford is seen to be all in the dark.
>
> Now which may be right or which may be wrong
> We must leave, for mine is a fallible song.
> I run from the Conflict the better the quicker,
> And leave the Dispute to the Farmer and Vicar

To arrange when the Farmer shall preach to the Town
In the Vicar's own Pulpit, and Surplice and Gown.
I shall come and the Church will be full, that is true,
And, till then, I bid Icomb and Burford Adieu.

The denomination of Baptists was not the only destination for disaffected Anglicans and Burgess was not Thomas West's only doctrinal opponent, he also found himself embroiled in exchanges with S. H., a Unitarian who challenged the scriptural authority for the doctrine of the Trinity.

Along with others Thomas West's wife Mary signed the chapel licence application to the Bishop of Worcester. She is represented in her husband's archives by a letter, sent by hand to a friend in London, which mysteriously found its way back to Icomb. Its presence here suggests that the Porter family may have caught the habit of keeping inconsequential letters as mementoes of relatives who died from their West kinfolk. Mary West's letter displays the perennial preoccupations of the wives and mothers of her day: sickness, death and servants. As women were given little or no tuition in reading and writing in the early 19th century, Mary West's idiosyncratic spelling is understandable. The letter, to Mrs Tidmarsh of 12 Paradise Row, Islington, London is dated 15 July 1829.

My dear Friend,

as Mr Mann was kind enough to offer to carry or send a letter I thought I would write a few lines to you hoping it will find you all quite well. I am happy to say that we are all very well at present thank God. My little girl is rather unhealthy, she is so liable to take cold she have most allways a cold upon her. She can't quite go alone she have had so many plunges of illness which makes her as she cannot gather strength very fast. She is very backwardly in cutting her teeth, she have but two as are quite throw and them punished her very much before they came throw. I am afraid she will suffer a great deal from them has her gums gets hard. I have been weaning of her this last week, had not very much trouble to do it. I thought she would eat her food better by so doing. I was very much pleased to hear of your having much good prospects. Mr Mann came and spent a day with us he told us that you had and was likely to have great connexions in the Laundry business. I hope and trust that everything will prosper with you whatever you take in hand to do. I was very sorry to hear of you dear partner's ill health and likewise you Child's. It must have been a great trial to you having so much to encounter with besides, but my dear friend we must not expect to go through this world without trials and it's a blessing for those who can say It is good for me that I have been in trouble.

I have also to acquaint you of the loss which I have experienced since I wrote to you last that is the Death of my dear father. He died soon after last Christmas, his illness was short. He lay ill but a week with inflammation upon the lungs. It was hard parting but I hope and trust that we shall meet again in heaven never to part more, knowing it was of the Lord, let him do what seemeth him good.

Eliza Merriman is also dead and young Steven

Reynolds of Slaughter, both in a decline. Eliza was become very penitent indeed before she died which must be a great blessing to her parents no doubt, but the prayers of her pious Mother had been heard. Mrs Clifford is very poorly still, it is the opinion of many that she is going in a decline. It was a great trial to her losing her Child and sister so near together. The Child was the same age to mine but it very often had fits and it died in a fit quite sudden which made it seem worse. Elizy Boulton said she should very much like to come and wait upon you if it was not for her family but she cannot because of that and Louisa as lives with me would come at Michaelmas if her mother was willing but she says she shan't go so far off. I dare say I shan't keep her again as she is got to take good wages and is fit for a better place. I can't think the reason why her Mother is so scilly not to let her go as it may be the making of her but she is determined not. She would be just the girl for you as you would trust her among anything and I should think it would be better for you to have one live with you in the house.

So no more from your sincere friend M West. I shall be very happy to hear from you.

Her little girl, Mary, survived her 'plunges of illness'. When the 1851 census was taken she was twenty-two and living with her parents at Icomb.

The date and provenance of the following frivolous verses, entitled *Crumbs of Comfort for the single ladies of Anywhere affectionately presented to them by the married Ladies of Somewhere,* which were handed down with the West papers, are unknown and their presence difficult to explain; but the burden of the piece, that 'courtship is one thing and wedlock another' is a comment on the state of matrimony that could have provoked wry smiles at any time in the past five hundred years.

> We're married – we're married and find, O! ye fair
> Our Castles of happiness built but in air.
> They were guarded by Cupids who promised to stay,
> Yet on Hymen's arrival, the rogues fled away.
> Our stores of felicity are but a joke
> And the bright luck of Hymen has ended in smoke.

> 'Tis true we no longer dread people who say
> Do look at that 'Old Maid' just over the way,
> But it's still more appalling for some one to sigh
> And remark 'how neglected is poor Mrs I'.
> That sweet Mrs A makes an excellent wife
> But her Husband's so cross she is weary of life.

> But a warm ardent lover was handsome young B
> When he courted the rich and accomplished Miss P.
> They were married last year and 'tis plain the connection
> Has brought his regard for her Cash to perfection.
> Sir John is delightful, his smiles are so bland,
> How envied the woman who gave him her hand;
> With this bright constellation abroad he may roam
> But a total eclipse shrouds his radiance at home.

Silly things! we won't think that these lords of Creation
Who when single beheld us with such admiration
Who swear and who vow their existence depends
On a look – on a word – that they'd compass the ends
Of the World, to procure us a moments repose,
Will as soon as we marry 'em turn up their nose
At our tears our entreaties and look on our grief
With a stoic philosophy passing belief.

Yet the gay Cavalier the gallant single man,
Who so kindly accepts all 'invites' that he can,
Who eats Papa's dinner and drinks Mama's tea
Hands 'dear Jane' to the carriage and flatters all three,
Will if caught by a fortune a figure or face
Prove that strange metamorphoses still can take place,
For a thousand and one constant nameless attentions
Once so freely bestowed, are now quite condescensions.

Superseded by 'Here Mrs—— take this seat
And just give me the stool which is under your feet',
The party selected because she'd be there,
Cards and Music neglected to stand by her chair,
Give place to a careless – 'You'll go to the Ms,
Say I'll come if I can but I promised some friends
To look in after dinner and then let me see
You'll return in the carriage, so cannot want me'.

Of presents the lover is always profuse
But the Husband discovers these things are no use.

240

'I must buy a dress love, to go to this ball'.
You must wear what you've got dear, or not go at all.
I'm sure Mr—— you can't wish me to stay
At home when I'm told it will be so gay.

Indeed Mrs—— you may go or remain,
It is not of that you will find me complain
But as for this dress you are talking about
I can't spare the money, that's flat so don't pout.

There once was a time Mr—— when you swore
My wishes should even – Pshaw, Madam, no more,
That nonsense is over, I've had time to cool,
Married men soon get tired of playing the fool;
I've just bought that hunter, those dogs, changed my gun
And must pay Snip the Tailor, that fellow's a Dun.
A little reflection I'm sure Mrs—— ask
Would shew you 'tis selfish to ask now for cash,
But so thoughtless you are, as I've told you before
'Twould drive any man mad, exit slamming the door.

Oh! Sisters – dear Sisters, your liberty prize,
In true 'single blessedness' stay if you're wise.
Leading Asses by dozens can never compare
With the lectures you'd suffer if led by a Bear,
And how'er you may flatter yourselves or each other
You'll find Courtship is one thing and Wedlock another.

Chapter Eleven

COTSWOLD FARMING
1790-1813

n the absence of family records we can turn to the *General View of the Agriculture of the County of Gloucester,* compiled by George Turner of Dowdeswell, and published in 1794, and the *General View of the County of Oxford* compiled by Arthur Young, and published nearly twenty years later, in 1813, to provide us with a picture of the practice of thinking farmers with the means to put their theories into practice in the stonebrash district on both sides of the county boundary.

> Probably no part of the kingdom [Turner thought] has been more improved within the last forty years than the Cotswold Hills . . . In the open field state, a crop and a fallow was the usual course. What is here called 'seven-field husbandry' now prevails; that is about a seventh part sainfoin – 'excellent grass' – and the remainder under the following routine: turnips, barley, seeds two years, wheat, oats.

Elsewhere in England, horses were replacing oxen as draught animals but, in the Cotswolds, oxen survived:

One team of horses is necessary for carrying out corn on our rough and hilly roads but, where more than one team is kept, oxen certainly are in every respect the most eligible. Where farms are large . . . a wooden house, fixed on a sledge is used to hold the ox harness, which, being drawn to the ground where the beasts are pastured, and as convenient as can be to their work, saves a great deal of time and unnecessary travelling.

The same cabins, if made with sparred bottoms and lids to open on each side, are very useful occasionally to keep calves in.

The native sheep of the district in their unimproved state was a small light-carcassed . . . animal . . . Since that time, the enclosing and better management taking place, and good rams being procured from Warwickshire and other Counties, the Cotswold Sheep have considerably improved in the weight of carcass and quantity of wool . . . although the wool was 'coarser than formerly'.

Twenty years later, Arthur Young's Oxford respondents included men like Mr Tuckwell of Signett, whose family was well known not only to Thomas West Porter and his sons but to earlier generations of the family: John Porter who died in 1721 married Elizabeth Tuckwell; her brothers were the overseers of his will. The rotation Mr Tuckwell described was similar to Turner's report: turnips; barley; two years of seeds; wheat; oats; peas and vetches. The 'seeds', Young explained, were clover and rye grass. Oxen were still favoured according to Tuckwell:

The breed is Hereford, bought at three years old . . . he
. . . thinks they should not be worked beyond seven, or at
most, eight years of age . . . sometimes has sold them to
graziers, but in general feeds them himself, yet has hardly
any permanent grass, as his is a stonebrash arable farm. In
working, thinks it of much consequence that they should
always have a little dry meat[58] with green food: some hay
cut into chaff night and morning. The same for fattening,
with turnips sliced into it, and finishing with swedes . . .
that they are much more profitable than horses, he has
not the shadow of a doubt . . . with him four oxen have
all this summer done more work than four horses.

But they need feeding.

To let them go back in winter and feed just when
they work is utterly unprofitable . . . In health and general
freedom from disease, they are superior to horses; he
does not even recollect having a lame ox.

A Burford respondent declared that sheep on the stonebrash farm were
'the grand object'.

---

[58] Fodder.

Chapter Twelve

FARMERS WHO LEFT WILLS

O f the men of the name of Porter who farmed in the Cotswolds before the nineteenth century, two stand out with greater definition than their kin: John Porter's father Humphry, who died in 1796, notable as the progenitor of twenty-six children and the author of a fascinating and masterly will; and this Humphry's grandfather, John, who died in 1700, the first man of whom we can say with confidence that he was ancestor of our line of Cotswold yeomen. The goods and chattels which John Porter of Sherborne left were recorded and valued in an inventory compiled on 23 September 1700 by Thomas Trinder and Joseph Trinder – two copies of it survive, along with his will, in the Gloucester County Record Office. One version of the inventory is written in a hand rooted in the medieval manuscript tradition, the other sits somewhere between the Italianate hand favoured by Elizabethan devotees of Renaissance culture and the copperplate in which Humphry Porter's will was inscribed in 1795.

The inventory of John Porter's goods begins, as inventories customarily do, with a valuation of his wearing apparel and the contents of his purse – £20 in money – and goes on to itemise the crops in his fields, his stock and implements and the contents of his

245

house, room by room. In the estimation of his appraisers, the sum total of John Porter's goods and chattels was £387 6s 8d.

John Porter farmed well over 100 acres in Sherbourne, and at the time of his death in 1700 he had sixty acres of barley, valued at £1 an acre; nine of wheat, worth £22 in all, seven of peas at £2 an acre; and fifteen of oats worth £13. He had harvested twenty-four loads of hay. John Porter owned 188 sheep 'of all sorts', eight cows, kept – as we shall see – for their milk; three heifers and three calves plus three hogs, presumably fattening for his own consumption. The principal products of his farm were grain, sheep and cheese: until the advent of the railways in the later nineteenth century the milk of most country cows was turned into cheese or long-keeping salted butter. This combination of sheep and corn, familiar to John Porter's Cotswold descendants for the next two centuries, did not yet incorporate the 'seeds' which formed such an important part of the farming regime of later generations. 'Seeds' came with enclosure, when the large 'open' fields which had been farmed cooperatively by the community were divided up and scattered holdings consolidated to form well-defined private fields cultivated by the owner or his tenant. Sherborne was enclosed in 1777.

As Abel Wonter of Gloucester, writing in 1714 observed,

> By enclosing their open fields and sowing the same with sainfoin, clovers, rye grass and suchlike seeds . . . thousands and thousands of acres of poor pitiful sorry ground, not [hardly] worth the ploughing and sowing with corn alone . . . being enclosed and sown with some of this seeds aforesaid, amongst their corn . . . bring forth so great an increase that the same land which before was

hardly worth 10 groats an acre will not be . . . let at three
times ten shillings an acre.

The appraisers of John Porter's goods recorded 'two suits of harness',
two long carts and a dung cart, two ploughs and five harrows but no
draught animals, neither oxen nor horse. Death brought a degree of
dislocation to any household and inventories should be read in this
light.

Having reviewed the fields, yard and outbuildings, the appraisers
moved indoors: the inventory portrays a farmhouse without the least
pretensions to fashion. They began their tour in 'the lower chamber',
the 'best bedroom', which contained a featherbed, bedstead and 'things
thereunto belonging'; a cupboard, a chair, a table board (the frame to
support it is not mentioned), a truckle bed (a low bed on castors which
could be trundled away under the bigger bedstead when it was not in
use) and a settle. The 'corn chamber' contained nothing but a bed –
best thought of as a mattress – and the bedstead and bedding which
went with it. In 'the chamber over the hall', the appraisers noted a third
bed, additional pillows and furniture which could be used for storage:
a cupboard, two boxes and a coffer. The chamber also contained
sheets, napkins and pillowcases, twenty-eight yards of cloth, a saddle
and a bridle. In farmhouses like John Porter's, items of agricultural
equipment are often found stored in bed chambers. Downstairs again,
in the hall, the main living space, they found a tableboard, a cupboard,
a form and three chairs. A fourth bed occupied the chamber over the
kitchen. The kitchen itself contained a pair of blankets, a malt mill, a
brewing vessel, and a 'sesston'. 'Sesston' probably represents an
attempt to get the local pronunciation of 'salting stone' down on paper
– salting stones were used in the process of preserving meat. There

was a salting tub in the buttery, along with seven barrels, a quantity of pewter – dishes, chamberpots and candlesticks – and brass including kettles, pots and a mortar for grinding; two warming pans, two spits and the andirons, or firedogs, on which the spits were hung, a fireshovel and tongs, smoothing irons, scales, a weighbeam and weights. Since John Porter paid tax on three hearths, it appears that only three of the rooms in the farmhouse had fireplaces. They were, in all likelihood, the hall, the chamber downstairs and the kitchen.

It is worth comparing John Porter's inventory with those of near contemporaries from the Vale of Gloucester. The goods and chattels in the possession of John Griffyth, Rector of Winterborne, appraised in 1698, were reckoned to be worth £378. Predictably, the rectory was more comfortable and stylish than John Porter's farmhouse. Mr Griffyth had a dining room, a parlour and a study. His furnishings included much more seating: a couch, leather chairs, rushseated chairs, settles, stools and cushions. He had books, two clocks, a watch and a small gold whistle on a chain. Such luxuries were not unknown in yeomen households in the Vale. Jacob Hollister, whose goods were appraised in 1689, was evidently an older man whose wealth consisted primarily of ready money, bonds and mortgages. He had 'books of several sorts', a clock and a dozen and a half of silver spoons. Humphrey, who died in 1796, was the first member of the Porter family to mention silver in his will. The abiding impression John Porter's inventory gives is of a thrifty man, ready to invest in the equipment necessary for the efficient running of his farm and household but uninterested in frills, a philosophy shared by his descendants into the twentieth century.

It is, however, not inventories but wills which are the prime source of evidence for the history of the Porter family from the middle of the seventeenth until the end of the eighteenth century. The wills

248

are the legacy to the Porter family's historians of three generations: John the elder of Sherborne (1642-1700); his sons John (1673-1721) of Eastleach Turville and Thomas (1675-1715) of Sherborne; and his grandsons (John the younger's sons) John (1703-1754), William (1705-1775), Thomas (1707-1729) and Humphry (1710-1796). Will-making was one of the rituals in which the dying took leave of this world and prepared themselves for the next. In the late seventeenth and earlier eighteenth centuries they were normally made by men and women who believed they were close to death.

The first will in our series, made by John Porter 'of Sherborne in the County of Gloucester, husbandman' on 27 June 1700 – we will return to the question of his status – 'being in good health and of sound and perfect mind and memory' but 'considering the frailty and uncertainty of this life' is exceptional, though not without parallel. By October, John Porter was dead – a circumstance which may have deterred his neighbours from 'tempting providence' by making a will, 'being in good health'. More typical is John I's son Thomas, who made his will in 1715, 'being sick and weak in body but of sound mind and memory'. One of John II's four will-making sons, Thomas, recorded his bequests in 1729 'being weak in body but of sound and disposing mind'. John III, who made his will in December 1748, a clear five years before his death, and William, who died a few weeks after his will was 'signed, sealed and published and declared' in January 1775, did not comment on their health. Humphrey, who made his will twenty years later in 1795, may have been erring on the side of optimism when he described himself at the age of eighty-five, as 'being in good health', although to judge from the clarity and sophistication of his bequests he was self-evidently 'of sound and disposing mind, memory and understanding'.

249

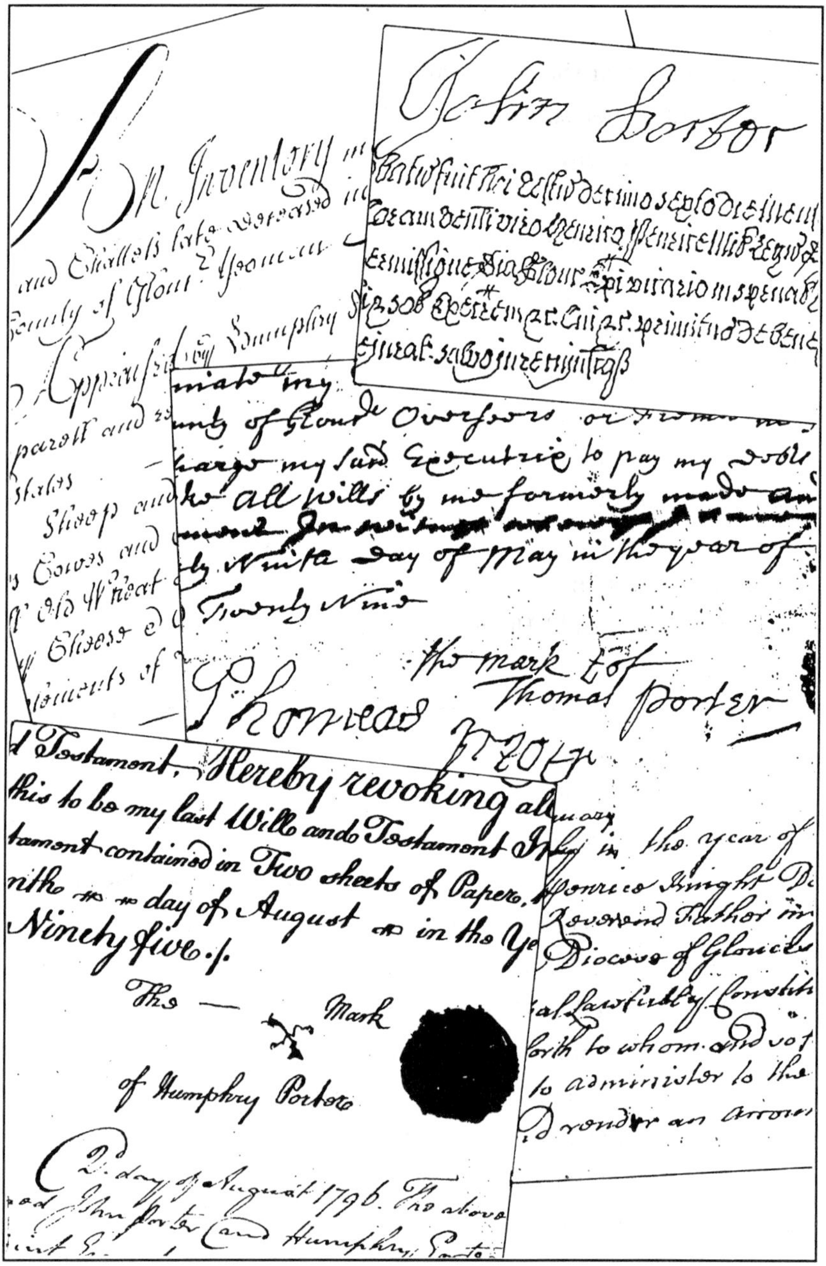
John Porter

An Inventory

and Chattels

Appraised

Sheep and

Cowes and

Old Wheat

Cheese

this to be my last Will and Testament

tament contained in Two sheets of Paper

day of August in the Ye

Ninety five.

The Mark of Humphry Porter

day of August 1796

John Porter and Humphry Porter

the mark of Thomas Porter

Thomas

to administer to the

render an Accoun

Claims of ill-health are often confirmed (as in the cases of both Thomases) by their shaky signatures. The younger Thomas's autograph is of particular interest: the scribe, whose hand is fluent, practised and confident without any pretension to calligraphic artistry, describes it as 'the mark of Thomas Porter'. The phrase 'the mark of Thomas Porter' is interrupted by a sign which resembles a lower-case 't', but, to the left, and below the inscription are the words 'Thomeas Prtotr' in large and very uncertain letters. Was this the work of Thomas, too ill to see and shape the familiar syllables of his name?

John I Porter of Sherborne, who may well have been able to read, though he could not write, made an emphatic mark, which resembles a capital I with a bar through the vertical stroke: a stylised and distinctive rendering of the initial capital of his given name. His grandson William made his mark with a confident and stylish 'W'. John III signed his name in full while old Humphry made crosses at the foot of each of the pages of his will in quavery and spluttering ink.

The testator's first bequest was normally of his soul. John I bequeathed his soul in an elaborate formula, 'into the hands of Almighty God my maker, trusting and relying on and through his mercy and the merits of my blessed Lord and Saviour, Jesus Christ, my blessed redeemer to find everlasting salvation'. Two decades later his son John II simply commended his 'soul to Almighty God who gave it, hoping to be saved by the merit of my Lord and Saviour Jesus Christ'. Thomas I, who died in 1715, made no mention of his soul, Thomas II commended his 'into the hands of All Mighty God, my creator'. It would be rash to assume that these wills accurately reflect their makers' beliefs: pious phrases were often supplied by the scribes who committed the testators' intentions to paper. The parson, the schoolmaster, the local landowner and his more substantial tenants

251

were frequently asked to write wills, adding to the grants and solemnity of the occasion the stamp of their personal authority and reputation.

John II's sons, John III, William and Humphry, plunged straight into the disposition of their worldly property. It is at this point in the will that the personality and personal history of its makers are most clearly expressed. Margaret Spufford, who used wills to explore the ways in which villagers in *Contrasting Communities* in seventeenth century Cambridgeshire 'thought and reacted' and 'the way [the] family group worked', argued that

> . . . the willmaking population was weighted by men leaving at least some children under age . . . Very few wills survive made by retired men who had established all their sons on the land, and married off all their daughters.

This thesis is supported by a couple of instances of long-lived men in later generations of the family: neither John Porter (1757-1851) nor William Lane, pictured on the dust jacket, who died in 1908 aged ninety-three, left wills. Of the will-making Porters, John I had a daughter of age but unmarried and John II and his sons, John III and Humphry, had some children under twenty-one. William was married but childless. The Thomases, perhaps sharing the scepticism displayed by the Apostle for whom they were named, were bachelors.

John I Porter, who died probably in his fifties in 1700, described himself in his will as 'husbandman', a form usually applied to smaller farmers. The appraisers who valued his goods did not make any observations on his occupation or status. The inventories of a group of Gloucestershire parishes to the north of Bristol – Almondsbury,

Alveston, Frampton Cotterell, Iron Acton, Stoke Gifford, Westerleigh and Winterbourne – are in print. Although comparisons, even within the boundaries of a single county, are to be treated with caution, John Porter proves to be many times better off than most of the husbandmen of the period; Simon Evans, George Bayly, Thomas Noble, Richard Tipper between them did not have goods to the value of his. Succeeding generations of the Porter family and their in-laws were confidently described as 'yeomen', the term applied to more substantial farmers who did not seek to emulate the domestic habits of the landed gentry. Not long before he died, John I Porter had purchased a lease of land from 'Walter Mathewes . . . yeoman'. The likelihood is that he was a man who had prospered through his own endeavours to the point at which he was sufficiently well-off to qualify as 'Yeoman', but that the memory of less prosperous days discouraged him from claiming the title for fear of having it challenged by the established yeomen of the locality.

John I's will supports Margaret Spufford's contentions that fledged children, adult sons and married daughters were normally provided for as they flew the nest (historians classify parental investment in educating and establishing the new generation as a life-time bequest) and that the will-maker was primarily concerned to secure the future of children still under his guardianship. John left the lease of the land he had 'lately purchased of Walter Mathewes of Sherborne . . . yeoman' to his son Thomas and, if Thomas predeceased him, to his unmarried daughter 'Sirsula' – Cecilia or Cicily as she was baptised. She was left £30 'to be paid her . . . within one year . . . after my decease, provided she be ruled by her mother and brothers in all things fit and reasonable' –primarily, of course, her matrimonial plans, but she died unmarried at the age of thirty-five only five years after her father's death. The Sherborne burial register shows that both she and her brother Thomas were 'buried in wool'. The Burial in Wool Act, which came into force in 1666, decreed that all coffins should be lined with woollen cloth and not linen, silk. This Act, repealed in 1814, was intended to help sheep farmers who were going through hard times.

Thomas and his brother John were to share their father's 'implements belonging to husbandry equally betwixt them, share and share alike'. His sons and his wife Susannah were to share the residue of his goods, chattels and credit, half to Susannah and half divided equally between John and Thomas. Readers familiar with the habits of landowners might be inclined to assume that Thomas was the elder brother. The order in which their names are recorded 'my two sons John Porter and Thomas Porter' argues to the contrary and the parish's baptismal register confirms that John was born in 1673 and Thomas in 1675.

Thomas died unmarried aged forty in 1715. He left £11 to the churchwardens and overseers of the poor of Sherborne 'to be placed out at interest . . . upon good security at ten shillings per annum and no more'. The interest was to be distributed to the 'necessitous and deserving poor of the parish from time to time for ever, yearly on the feast of the Nativity of our Lord God in the afternoon after divine service'. If the parish officers rejected the bequest, the sum of 40 shillings was to be distributed to the poor and the remaining £9 returned to Thomas's executor or to 'the eldest person of the name and family of the Porters, my relations'. The parish's response to the terms of Thomas's bequest is not recorded.

Thomas also left Ann Wayt, 'my servant', £10, desiring her to 'dwell with my mother as long as she [his mother] shall live'. (Susannah was probably sixty or thereabouts.) He left his house and three yardlands[59] – adding up to between 90 and 100 acres – to his elder brother John, who was charged with responsibility for paying over a legacy of £50 to their mother.

When John II died in 1721 in Eastleach Turville, none of his six sons was of age. He therefore appointed his brothers-in-law Humphry and Richard Tuckwell of Southrop, trustees and overseers of his will; his wife, their sister, was 'executrix'. He left his eldest son John III, born in 1703, £50 when he came of age, and his next brother William, born in 1705, the house in Pudding Lane in Eastleach Turville and the yardland which went with it. If William died before he married, the lease was to pass to his brother Thomas, born in 1707, and, if Thomas died unmarried, to Humphry, born in 1710, in turn. The bequests of money left to Thomas and Humphry and their younger brothers, Richard and Joseph, each assigned £220, suggest that the balance of probability was that William would live to marry (which he did). Elizabeth, the only daughter of this generation was left £320. If any of these children died before coming of age his or her portion was to be divided amongst the five younger ones or their survivors. Their mother, with a young family still to bring up, was to have the house called 'Simons' in Eastleach Turville and the yardland which went with it.

John's legacies add up to £1300. The inventory of his goods and chattels – a mere summary without any of the rich detail of his father's – was preserved along with his will. His total worth, assessed by neighbours whose judgement was respected in the community, was £1363, less funeral expenses and outstanding debts and the obligation to ensure that his widow Elizabeth was in a position to 'educate, breed

---

[59] Half a yardland, 15 or 20 acres, was traditionally reckoned to be the minimum holding on which a farming family could survive without earnings from another source.

up and maintain all [the] children with sufficient and competent meat, drink, lodging, schooling [and] apparel both linen and woollen'. It is a reminder that wills recorded intentions, not necessarily the means to realise them. Heirs frequently found their apparently generous portions eroded because they were burdened with the obligation to settle debts and honour bequests made to their brothers and sisters.

John II's son Thomas, born in 1707, dictated the terms of his will in 1729. The beneficiaries were his brothers – his sister Elizabeth was already dead; each was to receive £10. John, William and Humphry were by now of age, Richard, born in 1712, and Joseph, born in 1717, were to receive their legacies when they were twenty-one. Thomas's 'dear mother' was his executrix and residuary legatee.

John Porter III and his wife Anna had eight children born between 1725 and 1747: Anna, Jacob, Thomas, Samuel, Mary, Sarah, Fanny and Kitty. His will, proved in 1754, seems to have been intended to bring his twenty-three-year-old son Thomas to heel, for he instructed his brothers William and Humphry Porter and his brother-in-law John Allen to dispose of his estate in North Cerney, to pay the interest on the proceeds to his wife and, after her death, to divide the capital 'equally . . . among my children (except to my son Thomas) and that my son Jacob and my son Samuel shall each of them have £5 more than the others'. However, he went on, 'my will is that my Brother William Porter and my Brother Humphry Porter and my Brother-in-Law John Allen shall have a power to give to my son Thomas, if they shall think it proper, an equal share with all my children, except my son Jacob and my son Samuel'. Since John III did not modify his will in the last five years of his life, the rift between him and Thomas presumably remained unmended.

It seems likely that William Porter, who was seventy when he

256

made his will in 1775, had retired. He left his 'loving wife Hannah' the lands at Birdlip which she had brought to their marriage (unless protected by a trust, a wife's property, like her debts, became her husband's) and, in addition, £25 'yearly, to be paid to her quarterly, if required . . . out of my money and stock'. What remained at her death was to be divided equally between the children of his brothers John and Richard and the children of his brother Humphry's first marriage. Was it the size of Humphry's brood, still expanding in 1775, which persuaded William to impose this restriction in the hope of ensuring that those of his nieces and nephews who benefited under his will received legacies which were large enough to make a significant contribution to their welfare? The omission of the children of his fourth brother, Joseph, is unexplained. Joseph was evidently a favourite of his brother Humphry, who named no fewer than three of his sons for him and left Joseph's son John a token in his will.

The richest testament in this short series is, however, without doubt the will of Humphry Porter, born in 1710, who lived until he was eighty-six and fathered twenty-six children in his three marriages. Humphry's phenomenal paternity was not unparalleled. Indeed, Robert Shirley, first Earl Ferrers, born in 1650 had twenty-seven children, seventeen by his first wife and ten by his second. A bronze tablet at Nether Ettington in Warwickshire commemorates another prolific couple:

> Thomas Underhill of this town, Esquire and Elizabeth his wife who lived married together in perfect amity above 65 years and had issue between them XX children, viz: XIII sons and VII daughters, she died 24 June Anno Domini 1603 and he the 6 day of October next after.

Remarriage is the factor which unites the yeoman and the earl. Left a widower with young children at forty and again in his middle fifties, Humphry remarried to provide a surrogate mother for his family, a manager of the woman's side of the farm – the house, the dairy and the poultry yard – and for himself 'a loving wife', a companion at board and in his bed. Remarriage was the farmer's normal response to the death of a wife because her responsibilities were extensive and central to the farm's prosperity. At this date many farming households numbered servants-in-husbandry, as living-in farmworkers were known, among their members. The capable farmer's wife kept them well fed and well disciplined. No servant could be relied on to apply herself as diligently as a good wife. Besides, a servant took wages while a prudent marriage brought with it an injection of cash and kind.

The exceptional size of Humphry's family is explained by his repeated choice of women of childbearing age and by his – and one hopes his wives' – sustained appetite for the sexual aspects of marriage. By the time his last child, Catherine, was born in 1781, Humphry had achieved the biblical three score years and ten; he lived to see her almost grown up.

His will suggests that in 1795, the year before his death, Humphry Porter had five surviving children from his first marriage, the eldest sixty, the youngest in his mid-forties; three from the nine born in his second marriage: the eldest of them, John (from whom the last yeomen of the Cotswolds descend) was forty and the youngest an unmarried, but still marriageable, daughter of thirty. From his last marriage to his 'loving wife' Mary, there were four survivors, the eldest twenty-five years old.

Most of the children who predeceased him died within the first three years of their lives. Historians have suggested that parents responded to the deaths of infants with indifference. In support of this case, they cite, among other evidence, the reallocation of given names. Humphry Porter and his wives reused names. Among his fourteen sons there were three Humphrys, three Josephs, two Johns and two Richards; among his dozen daughters, three Catherines, two Anns and two Susannahs. It is worthy of note that no living child's name was duplicated.

We have no direct evidence of the public or private reaction to this sad procession of short lives. The church taught unquestioning submission to the will of God. Children who died were spared the anguish and uncertainties of life on earth. Once the little bodies racked with coughs, burning with fever, drained by diarrhoea were laid to rest, the dead babies could be imagined plump and playful in paradise. But behind the mask of public acceptance, we have enough testimony from fathers and mothers who articulated their grief to be sure that infant deaths, though frequent and expected, were the cause of great distress.

Names were markers. It was natural that Humphry should wish to hand on his own and to preserve the names used in earlier generations: William, John, Richard and Joseph were his brothers' names, Thomas his uncle's, Elizabeth his mother's and his sister's, Susannah his grandmother's. His wives brought with them opaque traditions from their own families. There were friends to remember.

Humphry's will is a distillation of the long and sumptuous history of his marriages and procreation. His first bequest went to the principal beneficiary of the will, Humphry, born in 1764, the eldest eligible son of his third marriage. He received a house and land at Eastleach Turville, identified, not by its size, but as 'John Wheeler's' old holding, plus a tenanted cottage in the village, £50 and a half-pint silver tankard.

YEOMEN OF THE COTSWOLDS

This major bequest taken care of, Humphry turned to the children of his first marriage. Priority went to William, born in 1739, the first of his sons to grow up, marry and have children of his own. By 1795 William was dead; his representatives were his daughters, neither of age, who were left £25 apiece. Next came their aunts, the three surviving daughters of his first marriage: Mary, wife of William Durham, received a legacy of £70, her sister Elizabeth, widow of Joseph Geering, and Sarah, wife of Jonathan Stevens were given £10 each; a later clause forgave debts Joseph Geering owed to his father-in-law. Their brothers, Richard, born in 1748, and Thomas, born in 1750, both mature men when their father died, received, respectively, £5 and a large silver spoon, and £20. The arrangements for the administration of Humphry's estate suggest that they were on good terms with their father and, we may confidently assume, had received their inheritance, among his lifetime bequests, when they struck out on their own. Thomas's daughter was left £20 in her own right; if she died unmarried underage, it was to be shared equally between her father and her uncle Richard.

The surviving sons of Humphry's second marriage were treated in a similar way. John had £50 and a silver tankard worth £7 (provided that he paid half its value to his younger brother Benjamin). Their sister Ann, still unmarried, was left £50, 'a large silver spoon marked 'A' and three silver teaspoons. Joseph, apparently the widower of their sister Joan, received £5.

Mary, 'loving wife' of Humphry's old age, was left £60 in money and 'the sacken bedstead' with its bedding – probably the bed she shared with Humphry.

The final group of major bequests relate to Mary's remaining children. Joseph, her eldest, born in 1771, was left £70 in trust, his younger brother Humphry and his older half brothers Richard and John were to be his trustees. The implication is clear: Joseph was disabled in some way that made him permanently incapable of either earning his living or of managing his own affairs. The youngest children were still under age, although David, born in 1775, was nearing his majority. He and his sister Catherine, born in 1781, were each alloted £50. If one died before reaching the age of twenty-one, the survivor was to have the whole of the capital and the interest due on it. However, since their guardians Richard, John and Humphry were empowered to 'make use of the whole or any part of the legacies . . . for or towards their maintenance and education of placing them out in the world,' the size of the nest egg they were to receive was very much dependent on their brothers' skill and goodwill.

After a last specific bequest of 'a mourning ring of one guinea's value . . . to my nephew John Porter, son of my brother Joseph Porter', Humphry assigned the remainder of his estate 'ready money, securities for money, goods, estate chattels, effects and personal estate' to his three sons Richard, John and Humphry 'to be equally divided between them, share and share alike'. John and Humphry were his executors. A note at the end of the will explains that Richard's was 'struck out' from the responsibility of executing his father's will 'on account of the said Richard Porter being a considerable Debtor to the said Testator.

The care with which Humphry Porter differentiated between the children of his three wives when he was apportioning his estate contrasts with the choice of sons representing each of his marriages to be his residuary legatees, 'share and share alike', and it may be that he had their mothers' dowries in mind when he assigned specific legacies to his surviving children.

Chapter Thirteen

TENUOUS LINKS

chain of evidence, comprised of public records and private papers, has enabled us to retrace the history of the Porter family through eight generations: from David Lane Porter, born at Crondall in Hampshire in 1934, to John Porter, husbandman of Sherborne in Gloucestershire, who died in 1700 and is buried in the churchyard at Eastleach Turville.

John Porter first appears in the Sherborne parish register as the father of William, baptised in 1667. Inside a year the baby and his mother Susannah were both dead. John and his second wife, also Susannah, were the parents of Cicily, born in 1670 and John II born in 1673 from whom the unbroken line of Cotswold yeomen descended. Twenty miles away, in 1670, in the parish of Mickleton, a family of the name of Porter vanished from the records. Edmund Porter, baptised in 1612, married Anne Ingrams in 1641; their son John was baptised the following year and their daughter Jane in 1646. Edmund's burial was recorded in 1670; Anne and the children left no further trace in the parish register. And, as we already know, in or before the year 1667, John Porter, a man of the right age to be the son of Anne and Edmund, turned up in Sherborne.

Although a leap of faith would have to be made to identify the John Porter who died at Sherborne in 1700 with the John Porter who

262

was born at Mickleton in 1642, it was a trail worth pursuing. Material in the County Record Office at Gloucester suggests that Edmund's parents were Alice, who died in 1637, and Thomas, who died in 1658; and that his grandparents were William, who died in 1601, and Margaret, who died three years later. The very unusual Christian name Grisigon, borne by a member of this family, raised the tempting possibility that these Porters were closely related to their much richer neighbours and namesakes, Anthony Porter of Aston-sub-Edge in Warwickshire, who died in 1557, and his wife Grizigona, daughter of Sir Edward Stradling. Might William have been their son?

There are two main objections to the identification. One is the difference in rank between the son and heir of Anthony Porter Esquire, a title formally reserved for the eldest sons of knights, and the William Porter who died in 1602 and described himself in his will as 'husbandman'. This William had no seal and could not sign his name. He was, admittedly, 'sick in body' but his mark, shaped like the cross of Lorraine with two horizontal members, bears no resemblance to the initial letter of either his Christian or his family name. His will makes it clear that he was a sheepman. His bequest to his oldest son John was 'a score of sheep or £8 at his choice'; and he left Anthony Beard, his daughter's son, 'a ewe and a lamb at May Day next'. His debts included the outstanding purchase price of sheep due to be settled 'at St James Eve next' and at 'Martinstide next'.

The other objection is the conclusion of the Heralds – who visited Warwickshire in 1619 to investigate claims to bear coats of arms – that William Porter, son of Anthony Porter and Grizigona, daughter of Edward Stradling, knight, died childless. However, the Heralds' *Visitation of Gloucestershire 1623* recorded that William son of Anthony had two sons and two daughters and died in great poverty in 1570.

J. H. Morrison accepted the former view and, in the course of his researches into the history of the Underhills, examined the descent of the Porter family of Aston-Sub-Edge. To quote Morrison:

> Anthony Porter of Chypyn Camden [as he is described in deeds] had acquired lands in Aston under Edge. Anthony's will, dated June 10 and proved at Gloucester on November 15, 1557 mentions his wife Grysygon, his daughters Katherine and Elizabeth, and his sons, William, Nykolles and Edmond; but William was buried at Aston-sub-Edge on February 4, 1570-1 leaving Nicholas the head of this, the senior, branch of the Porter family.

Anthony Porter is also shown as having both a younger brother as well as a son named William. Morrison's careful reconstruction is persuasive, though the failure to establish a firm link with these namesakes deprives our yeomen of the Cotswolds of a number of colourful kinsmen.

In *The Underhills of Warwickshire*, he quotes at length on the death of Anthony Porter's cousin Thomas Porter in 1557, which was the subject of a case in the Court of Star Chamber:

> Thomas Porter, late of Over Ettington in the county of Warwick, gentleman, being sore sick in his dwelling house at Ettington aforesaid of a certain fever . . . the same Thomas Porter, little dreading the fear of God, took a knife in his hands, and with the same knife then and there gave unto himself a great cut and grievous wounds overthwart his throat from one side of the neck to the

other, intending thereby willingly to have murdered and destroyed himself out of hand. Yet, nevertheless, the said Thomas Porter languished of the said wounds from the same day that he had so sore stricken and hurt himself unto the Monday the next following, upon the which day the same Thomas Porter of the said wound died.

Thomas Underhill testified that he had been summoned to the chamber where Thomas Porter lay.

The same Thomas Porter said to the same Thomas Underhill 'Ah Cousin Underhill, what a villain am I. I have cut mine own throat. I am damned.'

And the said Thomas Underhill said unto him, 'Ah, cousin, say not so. Be you well assured that God hath appointed you to be saved. Therefore ask mercy and you shall have it.'

. . . [The coroner's jury] found that he had died of an Act of God (his illness) and not of his wound. They are therefore charged with perjury. The jury reply that the wounds were only scratches, and that the cause of death was 'a certain fever called the new ague'. They add that the Underhills had an interest in contending that it was a case of suicide, because they had certain disputes with the executors, which would be favourably affected by such a verdict. The judgement of the Court was not preserved.

If we trace this line back we find that Anthony's father was William Porter who served as Serjeant-at-Arms under Henry VII and Henry VIII. His main responsibility was as an arresting officer – he was killed apparently in the overzealous execution of his duties in 1515. Certainly 'George Thokmarton of London . . . received a pardon for killing William Porter, serjeant at arms in self-defence in Foster Lane in London'.

William was the son of Richard Porter of Mickleton who set up a charity in 1512. The Richard Porter Trust still exists and owns the school, school house and allotment gounds in Mickleton and the rent from them is divided between the parish church and educational needs of the village children.

Richard's father, another William, died in 1480 and his grandfather Robert died in 1453. Both lived at Over Ettington, Warwickshire. Robert's brother William Porter was made Knight of the Bath by Henry IV in 1409. This order had been created by the king ten years earlier and was so called because of the bathing ceremony which took place when a knight was inaugurated – a symbol of his purity. (The last time Knights of the Bath were created in this ancient form was in 1661 at the Coronation of Charles II. The 'modern' Order of the Bath was created by George I in 1725.) William married Agnes, daughter of Sir Adam Fraunceys (Lord Mayor of London 1352-1354) and they lived in Colyweston, Northamptonshire; he founded the Grey Friars Monastery in Stamford in 1397 and was buried there, childless, in 1436. William and Robert were the eldest of the five sons of Robert Porter, who died at the end of the fourteenth century and is the earliest member of this line of Porters to be documented. Differing versions of the family tree describe him as being from Over Ettington, Nether Eatington, North Ellington or North Elrington, but all are likely to be part of what is now

Ettington, just south of Stratford-upon-Avon and only a few miles from Mickleton.

But if we accept Morrison's findings, the greatest sacrifice must surely be the loss of a clear kinship with the well-known Endymion Porter. Anthony Wood, the Oxford antiquary, not generally a writer of bland character sketches, described Endymion Porter as

> . . . beloved by two kings: James I for his admirable wit, and Charles I for his general learning, brave style, sweet temper, great experience, travels, and modern languages.

Endymion, born in 1587, was the son of Edmund Porter and his half-Spanish wife Angela, whose grandfather was Anthony's younger brother. Endymion grew up speaking Spanish as well as English. Indeed his career as a courtier began in Spain. When he returned to England, he entered the service of Edward Villiers and then moved to the household of Villiers' younger half-brother George, James I's favourite, later Duke of Buckingham. In 1620 he married Buckingham's niece Olivia Boteler.

As Buckingham's Spanish-speaking servant, Endymion was one of the supporting players in the farcical expedition to woo the Infanta in 1623 as a bride for the King's son Charles. The episode did him no harm. The disappointed suitor took him on as groom of the Bedchamber. He was a confidential servant of the King's and, as Sir John Finet, Master of Ceremonies at the Court of Charles I noted with irritation, undertook tasks 'which should have been [those of] an earl's son or a baron'.

At the cultivated Carolean court Endymion became a friend of painters and a patron of letters. Van Dyck's *Self-portrait with Endymion Porter* is in the Prado, Madrid, and his portrait of Olivia belongs to the Duke of Northumberland. Mrs Gervas Huxley owns Van Dyck's portrayal of Endymion and Olivia with three of their children. Endymion was also a friend of Rubens and owned his *St George and the Dragon,* which is now in the English Royal Collection. This is Rubens' only portrait of Charles, in which Henrietta Maria is the rescued princess to her husband's George.

But perhaps Endymion Porter is seen at his best as friend and patron of William Davenant, the son of an Oxford innkeeper who became Poet Laureate in 1638. In 1630 Davenant was struck down with syphilis. Rumour had it that he was dead. In this crisis only Endymion Porter and the Queen's physician Dr Cademan remained loyal. Davenant dedicated his most successful play, *The Wits,* to Endymion who had intervened to secure the licence for its first performance in 1634. Four years later Davenant dedicated *Madagascar and other poems* to Endymion, who was asked by the poet to write the 'frontispiece' for the collection, but, as he ruefully confided to the reader,

> . . . if he did know, but with what pains I make
> A verse, he'd pity then my wretched case
> For at the birth of each, I twist my face
> As if I drew a tooth: I blot and write
> Then look as pale as some that go to fight:
> With the whole kennel of the alphabet
> I hunt sometimes an hour, one rhyme to get . . .

Among Davenant's best and most frequently anthologised verses is

For the Lady, Olivia Porter.
A present, upon a New-yeares day

Goe! hunt the whiter Ermine! and present
His wealthy skin, as this dayes Tribute sent
To my Endimion's love; Though she be farre
More gently smooth, more soft than Ermines are!
Goe! Climbe that Rock! and when thou there hast found
A Starre, contracted in a Diamond,
Give it Endimion's Love; whose glorious Eyes
Darken the Starry Jewells of the Skies!
Goe! dive into the Southern Sea! and when
Th'ast found (to trouble the nice sight of Men)
A swelling Pearle; and such whose single worth
Boasts all the wonders which the Seas bring forth;
Give it Endimion's Love! whose ev'ry Teare
Would more enrich the skillfull Jeweller.
How I command! how slowly they obey!
The churlish Tartar will not hunt to day;
Nor will that lazy, sallow Indian strive
To climbe the Rock or that dull Negro dive.
Thus Poets like to Kings (by trust deceiv'd)
Give oftner what is heard of, than receiv'd.

Endymion's match with Olivia Boteler had flowered into a famously devoted marriage, in contrast to others negotiated by Buckingham for his numerous female kin. Often separated from his anxious wife and baby son George by his duties at Court, Endymion became an eloquent letter writer.

My only sweetheart [he wrote to Olivia]

The great desire I have to see thee keeps alive thine image in me, and the extraordinary love which I receive from thee makes me discover mine with as much zeal as my poor understanding will afford, for I am sure I do outlove you, and will be a precedent for all mankind if ever I have to show how a husband ought to love as good a wife. Be happy in all thou thinkest of me, if any deserts in me can make thee so, for be assured that I will never change. God bless the child and make him a Saint George, and let not your prayers be wanting for your true friend and loving husband

Endymion Porter

Olivia was often jealous of her husband and suspected him of being unfaithful, although he strongly denied it. In 1624 he wrote:

Since my coming into Spain I have received four letters from you, and the two first with so much kindness in them, as I thought my love rewarded; but the two last are so full of mistrusts and falsehoods, that I rather fear you have changed your affection than that you have any sure grounds for what you accuse me of in them, for as I hope for mercy at God's hands I neither kist nor touched any woman since I left you, and for the innkeeper's daughter at Boulogne, I was so far from kissing her, that as I hope to be saved I cannot remember that I saw any such woman . . . Good Olive, let me receive no more quarelling letters from you, for I desire but your love, it

270

being the thing that only affords me pleasure in this vile world. Send me word how the children do, and whether Charles [his second son] be black or fair, and who he is like.

Endymion often sent presents to his wife to assure her of his love: 'a jewel of diamonds worth some hundred pounds', 'a picture of Mary Magdalene with a pot of flowers by her' and 'two boxes of perfumes'. He also sent 'six little glass bottles with silver chains for little George'; that letter continued

I pray you send me word whether he hath ever a great tooth yet or no, and how many teeth little Charles hath ... I would have you cut George his hair somewhat short, and not to beat him overmuch. I hope you let him go bareheaded, for otherwise he will be so tender that upon every occasion you will have him sick.'

Earlier when he had heard that little George was ill he hoped it was nothing but 'breeding of teeth, and when they come forth he will be well.'

Reading his mother Angela Porter's letters, it is tempting to conclude that Endymion learned his letter-writing, like his Spanish, from her. The following is a fragment from a letter she sent Endymion; his children were staying with her in the country when London was dangerously full of plague in the summer of 1625.

I wish you could see me sitting at the table with my little chickens, on either side, in all my life I have not had such

271

an occupation to my content to see them in bed at night and get them up in the morning.

The little one is exactly like what you were when you were of his age, and if it were not tiring you, I would give you such a sermon . . . You may rest assured that you need not be anxious: This situation is healthy, and no care that can be bestowed upon them is wanting to keep them in health . . .

I will inform you respecting everything but I must now go and see my little ones to bed.

Your mother

Angela Porter

These delightful letters were, of course, the product of Endymion's absences. Robert Herrick commiserated with him trapped in the town, at court, or on diplomatic missions abroad.

Sweet country life, to such unknown.
Whose lives are others, not their own,
But serving courts and cities, be
Less happy, less enjoying thee . . .

Endymion Porter remained loyal to his master Charles I and suffered as a consequence. A year before the King was executed, Endymion was in exile in France. On 19th January 1648 he wrote from Paris to Edward Nicholas, secretary to the Admiralty:

I am a sad man to understand that your honour is reduced to want; but it is all our cases, for I am in so much

Endymion Porter with his wife and sons.

necessity, that were it not for an Irish barber, that was once my servant, I might have starved for want of bread. He hath lent me some monies, which will last me a fortnight longer, and then I shall be as much subject to misery as I was before. Here in our court no man looks on me and the Queen thinks I lost my estate for want of wit, rather than my loyalty to the King my master, but God be thanked I know my own heart, and am so satisfied in my own conscience, and were it to do again, I would as freely sacrifice all without hopes of reward as I have done this.

Endymion was permitted to return to London in November 1648; he died bankrupt in the following August. He was buried in St Martin-in-the Fields, London. Olivia lived to see the restoration of the monarchy and was buried beside her husband in December 1653.

Likenesses taken by Van Dyck and by William Dobson, the leading English portrait-painter of the day, represent Endymion as tow-haired, round-cheeked, bucolic. The impression is misleading. Endymion was a loyal courtier but, as a later age would put it, a false squire. The country activity with which Endymion is most clearly associated, the Cotswold Olympic Games, was an invented tradition, a choreographed expression of the Cotswold spirit, as conceived by an outsider. Robert Dover, whose creation the Games were, was born in Norfolk in the 1580s. He was called to the Bar but there is little evidence of his practising. To his contemporaries, this was laudable. He was epitomised as

Dover that his knowledge not employs
T'increase his neighbours' quarrels but their joys.

Kinship ties brought Dover to Gloucestershire – his sister's husband was appointed rector of Saintsbury in 1602. Anthony Wood, the Oxford antiquary, linked Endymion Porter with Dover's Games; he states that they were held on the Thursday and Friday after Whitsun

> . . . for 40 years, by one Robert Dover, an attorney of Barton-on-the Heath in Warwickshire, son of John Dover of Norfolk, who being full of activity, and of a generous, free and public spirit, did, with leave from King James, select a place on the Cotswold Hills in Gloucestershire whereon those games should be enacted. Endymion Porter Esq., a native of that County, a servant of the King, a person also of a most generous spirit, did, to encourage Dover, give him some of the King's old clothes with a hat, and feather and ruff, purposely to grace him and complete the solemnity. Dover was constantly there in person, well-mounted and accoutred, and was the chief director and manager of those Games, frequented by the Nobility and gentry (some of whom came sixty miles to see them) and wear Dover's yellow favours.

The great eyecatcher of the Games was the 'famous and admirable portable fabric of Dover Castle, her ordinance and artillery': the guns were real.

Dover's Games were contests of strength and skill. The horse and foot races, jumping and hammer throwing would find their place in today's sporting calendar. Leap-frog, tumbling and walking on hands have been relegated to the playground and the circus ring. Tilting the quintain, a weighted sack suspended on a sword, guaranteed to knock

275

the less than artful contender from his horse is a lost skill. Many of the other competitions were violent and dangerous: wrestling and shin-kicking, for example. The less athletically inclined played cards or chess.

In 1636 the 'Yeerley Celebration of Mr Robert Dover's Olimpick Games upon Cotswold Hills', was itself commemorated in print with the publication of *Annalia Dubrensia*, a collection of complimentary verses written by men known as poets – William Davenant, Ben Johnson, Michael Drayton – a galaxy of gentlemen, many of them Oxford-educated, and one woman. As befitting what she described as 'Lady Modesty', she hid behind 'the name of a sirinx', the nymph who was transmuted into the reed from which Pan made his pipes.

The first series of the Cotswold Olympics ended with

> . . . the rascally rebellion that was begun by the Presbyterians, which gave a stop to their proceedings and spoiled all that was generous and ingenious elsewhere.

The Games were revived more than once after the Restoration. In the early 1800s their chief promoters were the local innkeepers. By the middle of the century they were attracting 'the lowest scum . . . of Birmingham and Oxford'. Their powerful patrons had deserted, 'no gentlemen of the neighbourhood attended them'. In 1853 'the scene of the Cotswold Games was finally ploughed up'. It is difficult to imagine Thomas West, his sister Mary or her husband Humphrey Porter not approving of this decision.

In the 1920s, a few years after Graham Lane Porter, his wife Edith and their children migrated from Holwell to a farm in Hampshire, Dover's Hill became the property of the National Trust. Trevelyan, writing in 1929, singled out the preservation of the natural amphitheatre which had been the site of Dover's Cotswold Olympics as one of the Trust's recent 'victories'.

Three hundred years separate the letter Angela Porter wrote to reassure her son Endymion that all was well with the children he had left in her care, from the letter Sarah Jane Butler wrote to reassure her daughter Edith that her baby son was thriving; not only do they share an intention, but they also choose the same way of getting it across, calling up a picture of the children engaged in the comforting routines of everyday life, playing or at the dinner table. The same worries that concern modern day parents were also an anxiety to our forefathers; babies' teething troubles were mentioned by Endymion in the 1620s, by Mary West two hundred years later and by Sarah Jane Butler in 1913.

It is diaries and letters such as these which give us the best access to evidence of shared or, equally illuminating, contrasting responses to similar circumstances and events of different generations. Like the National Trust's property at Dover's Hill, these documents are part of a common heritage, a history which, in a sense belongs to us all. This was indeed the instinct which led Gerald Porter to incorporate events and characters from the national past in his memorial book *Plum Money* and, in particular, to imagine the night on which William Tyndale, translator of the Bible, sought and found refuge with the household at Manor Farm, Holwell.

Graham Porter, aged 101, 1982.

A FINAL NOTE

lthough his name does not appear on the title page, this book belongs, above all, to Graham Porter (1881-1983). It was his reminiscences which first stirred interest in compiling a comprehensive history of the family, and his attention to detail and the accuracy of his memory which meant that names and facts could be put to the faces and places captured in Victorian and Edwardian family portraits. Many of the photographs reproduced in *Yeomen of the Cotswolds* carry on their reverse captions in the meticulous copperplate script which Graham Porter learned as a boy in the 1880s. Without these attributions, the photographs would have remained simply a box of miscellaneous visual delights. His identifications make them something more than quaint, decorative bygones. But how much more valuable they would be if their subjects had annotated them.

Many of us, whether we recognise it or not, are archivists responsible for collections of photographs, documents and ephemera. Our grandchildren and great-grandchildren will puzzle over them – unless we take our posterity seriously enough to answer those questions historians so often ask in vain when they interrogate material from times past: who? where? when? and, above all, why?

SOURCES & SUGGESTED FURTHER READING

Beer, Patricia, *Mrs Beer's House*, Anthony Mott, 1984

Brill, Edith, *Life and Tradition on the Cotswolds*, Dent, 1973

Campbell, Mildred, *The English Yeoman Under Elizabeth and the Early Stuarts*, Yale University Press, 1942

Edmond, Mary, *Rare Sir William Davenant, Poet Laureate, Playwright, Civil War General, Restoration Theatre Manager,* Manchester University Press, 1987

Gosse, Edmund, *Father and Son,* Alan Sutton, 1984

Gretton, Mary Sturge, *Burford Past and Present*, Faber & Faber, editions 1920, 1929, 1940

Hall, Sir Alfred, *A Pilgrimage of English Farming*, reprinted from *The Times,* London, 1913

Hey, David, *The Oxford Guide to Family History*, O.U.P., 1993

Huxley, Gervas, *Endymion Porter, The Life of a Courtier, 1587-1649*, London, 1959

Kendall, Sam, *Farming Memoirs of a West Country Yeoman*, London, 1944

Massingham, H. J., *Shepherd's Country: A Record of the Crafts and People of the Hills,* London, 1938

Miller, Celia (ed.), *Rain and Ruin: The Diary of an Oxfordshire Farmer, John Simpson Calvertt, 1875-1900*, Alan Sutton, 1983

Mingay, G. E. (ed.), *The Victorian Countryside*, Two Volumes, Routledge and Kegan Paul, 1981

Mingay, G. E., *A Social History of the English Countryside*, Routledge, 1990

Moore, John S., *The Goods and Chattels of Our Forefathers: Frampton Cotterell and District Probate Inventories 1539-1804*, Philimore, 1977

Moxon, Stanley, *Umbrella Frames 1848-1948, A Fox Centenary,* Stocksbridge, 1949

Morrison, J. H., *The Underhills of Warwickshire, Their Ancestry from the Thirteenth Century and their Descendants in England,* Cambridge, 1932

Orr, John, *Agriculture in Oxford: A Survey Made on Behalf of the Institute for Research in Agricultural Economics,* University of Oxford, 1916

Pryce, W. T. R. (ed.), *From Family History to Community History,* Two Volumes, C.U.P. in association with the Open University Press, 1994

Rogers, Colin D., *The Family Tree Detective: A Manual for Analysing and Solving Genealogical Problems in England and Wales, 1538 to the Present Day,* Manchester University Press, 1983

Rogers, Colin D., and John H. Smith, *Local Family History in England 1538-1914,* Manchester University Press., 1991

Rowntree, B. S., and May Kendall, *How the Labourer Lives: A Study of the Rural Labour Problem,* London, 1913

Samuel, Raphael (ed.), *Quarry Roughs: Life and Labour in Headington Quarry 1860-1920, An Essay in Oral History* printed in *Village Life and Labour,* Routledge and Kegan Paul, 1975

Spufford, Margaret, *Contrasting Communities: English Villagers in the Sixteenth and Seventeenth Centuries,* C.U.P., 1979

Thompson, Flora, *Lark Rise,* London, 1939. Currently in print as *The Illustrated Lark Rise to Candleford: A Trilogy,* abridged by Julian Shuckburgh , Century, 1991

Whetham, Edith (ed.), *The Agrarian History of England and Wales,* Volume VIII 1914-1939, C.U.P., 1978

281

$\mathcal{I}nd\varepsilon x$